DEADLY
DIVORCES

DEADLY DIVORCES

TWELVE TRUE STORIES OF MARRIAGES THAT ENDED IN MURDER

TAMMY COHEN

JOHN BLAKE

Published by John Blake Publishing Ltd,
3 Bramber Court, 2 Bramber Road,
London W14 9PB, England

www.blake.co.uk

First published in paperback in 2007

ISBN 978 1 84454 425 7

British Library Cataloguing-in-Publication Data:

A catalogue record for this book is available from the British Library.

Design by www.envydesign.co.uk

Printed and bound in Great Britain by Creative Print and Design, Ebbw Vales, Wales

1 3 5 7 9 10 8 6 4 2

Papers used by John Blake Publishing are natural, recyclable products made from wood
grown in sustainable forests. The manufacturing processes conform to the
environmental regulations of the country of origin.

Every attempt has been made to contact the relevant copyright-holders, but some were
unobtainable. We would be grateful if the appropriate people could contact us.

The events recounted throughout this book are based on true stories, some
of which may have been reported locally, nationally or internationally. Great care has
been taken to ensure their accuracy and factual integrity. Notwithstanding this,
certain accounts may vary from others when being retold, as permitted by the
freedom of discretion, the nature of poetic licence and dramatic effect and
where considered prudent for legal reasons.

CONTENTS

INTRODUCTION

Few things decimate a person quite like divorce. The oft-quoted statistic that divorce is the second most traumatic life event after the death of a member of one's family is misleading, for with death comes its own inevitable closure. Divorce, which can feel like the slow, tortuous disembowelling of a marriage, has no such finality. Though you might grieve for the life you had, for the person you lost, there is no body to bury ritualistically and no gravestone at which to unleash your feelings and weep. Instead the once-loved partner who has carved up your finances, your family life, your sense of self-worth, your very heart is still walking and breathing and a daily testament to the failure of your dreams.

Two out of five marriages currently end in divorce but it would be dangerous to allow the commonplaceness of divorce to negate its terrifying power and impact. It's a battlefield in which the three most primordial human obsessions – love, sex and money – become inextricably and dangerously intertwined. The stakes are high and the spoils of war deeply symbolic: children sometimes, not to mention status and home.

The truth is that divorce cuts to the very bone of a relationship exposing the ugly, bleeding flesh we normally try so hard to cover up. Marital homes purchased with hope and optimism become pressure cookers of building tension as accusations fly and barely formed emotions are ripped from deep within us in all their raw, howling intensity.

A recent poll by insidedivorce.com found that nearly one in five British couples admit to being on the brink of splitting up. That's a huge percentage of people riding the emotional rollercoaster of marital breakdown. When you factor in the discovery that infidelity, with its poisonous legacy of betrayal and bitterness, is the biggest single trigger for divorce, you start to build up some understanding of the extent of the devastation currently taking place behind closed doors.

Divorce tears at the very fabric of who we are and how – sometimes even why – we live. It's like a giant shredder from which our past life emerges in tatters; it pits lover against lover, parent against parent in a battle in which there are no rules, no protective clothing, no referees and no real winners. Recent years have seen some acrimonious and very public celebrity break-ups from Sir Paul and Heather McCartney to Britney Spears and Kevin Federline. These high-profile divorce cases merely prove fame is no protection against the vitriol released when a marriage is in meltdown. Divorce is, if nothing else, a great leveller.

With emotions running high, it's not surprising that the breakdown of a marriage can result in violence and sometimes even in death. Crimes of passion may no longer be recognised in law but would certainly be understood by many people who have undergone a traumatic split. Less easy to identify with are crimes that are planned out meticulously and methodically over the time it takes for a relationship to unravel. Do these count as temporary insanity or cold-blooded execution?

'Each man kills the thing he loves,' Oscar Wilde tellingly wrote. Certainly most of the crimes detailed in this book bear testament to that most poignant of sentiments. Love isn't always selfless or benign. It can be violent, possessive, exclusive and even predatory – and when it is threatened, it can also be deadly.

CHAPTER ONE

'SO YOU'VE COME TO SHOOT ME?'

Some days Rena Salmon could not believe her luck. Some days she would gaze around her £400,000 home in the affluent Berkshire village of Great Shefford, listening to her son and daughter laughing with their school friends in a different part of the house, and she'd wonder yet again how on earth she'd managed to end up there.

Great Shefford is prime commuter belt territory; near to Reading and Newbury, and not too far from London itself. Its picturesque cottages, good schools and country air make it a magnet for stockbrokers, solicitors and anyone else who dreams of a rural-style life with all city amenities close by – oh, and who can afford the hefty price-tag that property there commands. Luckily money wasn't a problem for

Rena because her husband Paul made a fortune as an IT consultant. Rena got to swan around in a fancy Merc and to take holidays at their seaside home in Dorset with its own private section of beach. Not bad for a woman who'd run away from home at the age of 13 and had spent most of her teenage years in Care. No wonder she sometimes had to give herself a good hard pinch to make sure this was actually real.

Born in Birmingham on 20 February 1960, Rena Beyum Uddin had not had the easiest of starts. Depending on who you talked to, you'd get a slightly different version of what childhood was like in the Uddin household, but let's just say none of the accounts would put you in mind of the Waltons. The story Rena and her sister Sabeya told was that their mother had been a prostitute; first in Birmingham and then Burnley. Growing up, they said, the house had been full of dirty old men, all clients of their mother's. Both Rena and Sabeya had dark skin, apparently a legacy of their different Asian fathers. This physical characteristic was a constant source of irritation to their mother, claimed the women, and she'd regularly scrub them roughly with a mixture of bleach and scouring powder to lighten their skin and referred to them as 'black bastards'.

Imagine what such a childhood would do to an impressionable young girl. Consider the daily beatings your ego and sense of self would sustain. Think how you'd shrivel inside and start hating your reflection in the mirror;

imagine how you'd come to believe that no one would ever love you, that you'd never be worthy of respect or affection. Picture how little hope you'd hold out of ever getting away from that situation, of ever being allowed anything 'better'.

Living in a series of foster homes and children's homes from the age of 13 hadn't done much either for Rena's fragile self-esteem. What message does that background send to a girl whose faith in people is already so tarnished? That nothing is permanent, what appears to be security can be whisked away at a moment's notice, that it's a cruel world and you have to hang onto what's yours because there's always someone else behind you waiting to snatch it away, leaving you with nothing.

But Rena's luck – or rather the lack of it – changed when she joined the Army. Here finally was her opportunity to belong to a group; almost a 'family' that would always take care of her in the way her real family had failed to do. After so many years of feeling like she didn't have the right clothes, of always sensing she was second best, Rena was proud to put on smart uniform everyday, finally to fit in.

She trained as a Data Telecoms Operator and in 1980 was posted to Northern Ireland. For many servicemen and women being sent to a place where hostility and tension seemed to hang heavy in the grey skies overhead would have constituted a nightmare posting, but for Rena it was the start of a dream life because it was here that she first met Paul Salmon. Paul was a technician with the Royal Signals. With his clear, sparkling eyes, curly brown hair and easy charm, he was the kind of man Rena Salmon had never imagined might actually be interested in her. But over time, the two struck up a friendship that deepened into romance.

There was only one slight blot on the pages of this fairy tale – Paul was already married. However, he wasn't going to let a little thing like that get in the way of a blossoming love affair. He set about getting divorced and in 1985 he and Rena tied the knot. For the girl who'd always felt unloved and unwanted; who'd been brought up to think she wasn't good enough, it was a day she thought she'd never see. At last she had found someone who loved her for who she was and didn't want to change her. After taking her vows, she silently added a couple of her own: that she would love this man forever and she would never let anything come between them.

Every new bride experiences that thrill of being reborn – of feeling as if she is starting out on a new life with the man she loves. For Rena Salmon, this sensation was even stronger than most. Her old life had been one of hardship and neglect. She wanted to put it far behind her. This new life was the real life where the true Rena would have a chance to come forward, shine and grow. And it was all down to Paul. With him by her side, at last she could find the happiness and security that had always eluded her.

When her son was born in 1989 and followed by a daughter in 1992, Rena's fairy tale seemed complete. She threw herself into being a perfect mum, showering on her own children the love and affection she herself had been denied. Everything she'd always thought lacking in herself, she now invested in her children. They would have the childhood she'd only ever seen in films – the meals out, the trips to the cinema, the family dinners. Gazing down at their sleeping bodies, she promised herself they would never come to harm and that as long as she lived she'd strive to give them the stability children so desperately need.

While Rena was delighted with the emotional riches married life had given her, it also didn't hurt that materially she now had everything she could wish for. In civilian life Paul had found a niche as a high earning IT consultant and within a short time he was earning over £80,000 a year. Rena too started working full time two years after her daughter's birth. For the first time in her life she didn't want for anything: she had beautiful clothes and expensive cars; she went on shopping sprees to New York and took pleasure in buying herself nice things. Finally she was starting to let herself believe that she was worth it.

In 1998 the Salmons moved to the Great Shefford house. Rena was in her element, buying things for the house, creating the home she'd never had. She started to make friends in the neighbourhood; mostly women she met while dropping off or picking up her kids from school. One of these new friends was Lorna Rodrigues.

Although Lorna was seven years younger, the two just seemed to click. Lorna was energetic and fun to be around, the perfect pick-me-up for the more reserved older woman. Also, being married to a mixed-race Australian meant that Lorna was more multi-culturally aware than most of the people in this predominantly white middle-class town.

Lorna ran a successful beauty salon in Chiswick, west London and her husband Keith was a computer expert but at weekends they liked to spend time with their two daughters and other local families. It wasn't long before the Salmons and the Rodrigues began socialising outside school, enjoying dinner parties and barbecues at one another's houses; it was the kind of friendship Rena had always craved. She felt as though she could talk to Lorna about anything, including her worries about her marriage.

You see, Rena had begun to feel as if Paul was slipping away from her. It had started a few years before when she'd developed chronic back pain. Depressed and largely immobile, she started to binge eat and the weight had piled on. Paul, a fitness fanatic who always took pride in keeping in shape, had tried to encourage her to eat properly: 'Come on, you'll feel better if you just eat a little healthier,' he'd coax her. But one of the most damaging legacies of Rena's past was the way emotion always crowded out reason in stressful situations. Lacking any coping skills for dealing with pressure, she'd give in to her emotions. She knew she shouldn't stuff herself with food —she knew it was driving her husband away — but that very knowledge made the urge to eat even stronger.

Paul became increasingly distant. He stayed out late after work and seemed to have lost interest in her. Their once solid marriage was looking more and more fragile. Rena had hoped that moving to a new area would provide the fresh start they needed but while they both loved being there, it hadn't brought them closer.

'Our sex life has really gone down hill,' Rena confided to Lorna one day. Lorna was immediately sympathetic: 'What you need is something to spice things up in the bedroom,' she advised her new friend. But the sexy new underwear Rena splashed out on did nothing to stop the rot in her marriage. Paul simply didn't seem interested. During the week he was always at work and then at weekends he'd go out drinking with friends. She never knew where he was and though she suspected there were other women, she chose to ignore this rather than face her suspicions head on. The couple became locked into that cycle that most unhappy marriages come to know so well. One partner feels the other is pulling away so they become clingy and emotionally needy which in turn pushes the other partner still further away. The word 'divorce' began to loom large in Rena Salmon's fears.

She couldn't accept it; wouldn't accept it. Here was a woman who'd been rejected all her life. Finally she'd found someone who made her feel wanted and accepted. She'd made a life where she had a place and a value. Not only this but she'd invested all her emotional reserves, all the love she kept inside her through the dark years in her family and her man. She couldn't live without him – he *had* to stay with her. She'd change, she'd get thinner; she'd start being more outgoing and less clingy. She'd do anything, *anything* to keep him.

What could be crueller than a once loving relationship where one partner has lost interest? What could hurt more than looking into clear eyes that were once full of love to meet only indifference? Rena knew she'd let herself get overweight and she knew her emotional dependence was driving her husband away. But she didn't know what to do about it. Thank goodness she had Lorna to turn to in those lonely moments when it all seemed too much to bear.

But by the end of 2001, Lorna Rodrigues had other things occupying her mind apart from her friend's marital problems: she had a new lover. Even thinking the words sent a thrill through her. She hadn't been looking for it, hadn't ever thought about it but then along came this man saying all the right things and wham! She'd fallen into this full-blown love affair. There were only two problems (i) he was married and (ii) he was married to her best friend.

Paul Salmon had taken to Lorna the first time he met her.

She was so much fun plus she was a successful businesswoman and as the owner of a beauty salon she was always immaculately turned out – the exact opposite of his own wife, in fact. The more time Paul spent with Lorna, the more he couldn't help comparing her to Rena. Why couldn't Rena be more independent? Why did she always have to ask him where he was going and what he was doing? Why did the little things she did irritate him so much?

He started imagining what life would be like if it was Lorna he went home to at night instead of Rena, if it was Lorna he watched undressing before bed and if it was Lorna's body laying beside him at night. Soon thoughts of the younger woman began to obsess him. She was never far from his mind and he knew he had to tell her how he felt.

In November 2001, after a series of chance meetings, Paul phoned Lorna and said he'd like to see her. They arranged a meeting and, with his heart pounding, he confessed his feelings. This was the moment everything else hinged on, the moment that set in motion the chain of events that came after. Did Lorna hesitate? Torn between her undeniable attraction to Paul and her loyalty to his wife, did she struggle to suppress her feelings for this married man? If the battle between guilt and temptation that waged inside Lorna Rodrigues had gone a different way, so much tragedy might have been avoided. But she was flattered. Who wouldn't be? She loved the idea that this successful, handsome man found her attractive. Sure, it was a shame they were both married but then no one else needed to find out, did they?

Just a month later, Keith Rodrigues was looking through his wife's email account when he came across a message that made his heart freeze:

> 'It was great to be with you,' it read, 'to be able to hold you.'

We all think we know how we'd react when faced with a spouse's infidelity – yell, scream, throw things, storm out. Yet for many of us the only course of action is no action, just an immediate paralysis, a wall of denial and disbelief that springs up around the heart to protect it from cracking right down the middle. Keith Rodrigues stood rooted to the spot. It couldn't be true. Surely she wouldn't do that to him; what about the children, too? What about the family they'd so carefully and so lovingly built up? Would Lorna really want to jeopardise all that? In shock he scrolled through the message again and again. There was no mistake, there could be no innocent explanation: his wife was having an affair.

Keith Rodrigues loved his wife; he adored her, in fact. Sure they'd had their problems over the years but what couple hadn't? He never imagined she would have betrayed him like this and with someone they both knew. It was a real kick in the teeth for the unassuming family man. What had he done that was so wrong that it sent her running into another man's arms? Hadn't he been enough for her?

Any spouse discovering infidelity feels inadequate. Men in particular can feel like sexual failures, as if they haven't been man enough to please their wives. They become haunted by visions of their spouse in bed with someone else, so-called 'mind movies' of the lovers having sex play incessantly through their heads as if on continuous loop. Everyone reacts in different ways. Some are angry, some disbelieving, others just broken but all they want the same result: they want it to stop.

When a trembling Keith Rodrigues confronted his wife in December 2001, deep down he knew what he wanted. More than anything he wanted Paul Salmon off the scene and his family to stay together. The couple talked long into the night. Keith was adamant Rena should know what had been going on for she was as much betrayed as he was. She had a right to be told, to know what kind of man she was living with. Plus, once Rena knew, she'd be able to keep an eye on what Paul was getting up to and maybe he'd start to leave Lorna alone.

Keith was all for telling Rena right away but Lorna managed to convince him to hold off. It was December, Christmas was round the corner and Rena wasn't the kind of woman who'd be able to hide her feelings. What kind of festive season were the four children involved going to have if the adults around them were constantly rowing and crying? What sort of holiday was Rena herself going to have? This news was going to rip the very heart out of her carefully constructed family life. Surely he could find it in himself to give her the greatest gift of all – peace of mind – even if it was all a temporary illusion?

In the end kind-hearted Keith Rodrigues agreed to postpone dropping the bombshell – but not for long. In January 2002 he gave Rena and Paul's daughter a lift home from school and he came in to see Rena for a chat. Taking a deep breath, he told her as gently as he could: 'Lorna's having an affair.' Rena was immediately sympathetic. The poor man. She could see how upset and broken he was. 'It'll be all right,' she reassured Keith, putting her arms around him. He in turn put his arms around her waist, knowing that what he was about to say would shatter her world.

'It's not the worst bit,' he told her. 'It's Paul.' At that moment Rena felt like she couldn't breathe: Paul was cheating on her and with one of her closest friends. She couldn't take it in. Yes, she'd known her marriage was shaky but she'd told herself they'd get through it. Every couple had bad patches, didn't they? She and Paul were a team: they had two amazing children, they'd built up a great life for themselves. He wasn't about to throw all that away, was he? Until now Rena managed to plaster over the cracks in her crumbling marriage but Keith Rodrigues' news took a sledgehammer to all that.

'I don't believe it,' she gasped. If someone had physically punched her in the stomach she couldn't have felt more pain than she did now. It was as if a hand had seized hold of her insides and was twisting them cruelly round and round. Not Paul, not Lorna – it couldn't be true.

Suddenly all the years fell away and once again she was the child no one wanted; the one who'd never been attractive enough or good enough; the one who'd learned to expect rejection as her birthright. She was the dark-skinned, dark-haired girl whose mother had made her feel ugly and who'd grown up feeling less worthy, less loveable than the blue-eyed, fair-skinned children all around her. Blue eyed like Lorna, fair skinned like Lorna. Trembling, her emotions rushing through her like an unstoppable force, she picked up the phone and dialled her husband's mobile.

Paul Salmon was sitting at his desk at work when the phone rang. As soon as he answered, he knew something was very wrong. Rena's voice was raw with grief and rage; also a hysterical venom. 'You bastard!' she screamed. 'You cheating, lying bastard! You'll never see your kids again!' Undeterred, Paul told his wife he'd fallen in love with Lorna and wasn't about to give her up.

Knowledge of infidelity does strange things to the mind. You start relentlessly re-examining the past and in the brutal light of this new discovery, nothing now looks the same. Events that were happy in retrospect seem to be hollow at the core. Loving words once spoken are now stripped of all meaning. The happy family picture has a dark shadow hanging over it. Even logical, well-balanced people can go dangerously off the rails confronted with a spouse's affair. What hope then for a fragile and emotionally abused woman such as Rena?

For both couples it was a terrible time. The recriminations were endless, every conversation punctuated by 'How could you?' There were tears and arguments; doors were slammed and voices raised. In the end the Rodrigues made a drastic decision: they would move to Australia and start life afresh away from this mess. They'd work on being a family again, just as they had before. Keith was convinced he could make Lorna happy just as long as she was as far away as possible from Paul Salmon.

In January 2002 the Rodrigues family left for their new life and that should have been the end of the matter. But anyone who has ever been involved in an illicit love affair will tell you that sometimes the emotional high it produces is stronger than any drug and breaking contact is like breaking with an addiction, an addiction thousands of miles can't cure.

Lorna and Paul never quite managed to break free of one another. By this stage they probably didn't want to. Each had found in the other something missing in their marriage. Now they'd found it, they didn't want to lose it again. Before long they were speaking on the phone.

'Right country, wrong man,' Lorna told Paul in one call.

Just months after setting out for her new life in Perth, she was back in the UK – alone.

Rena thought she'd rid herself of the threat that hung over her marriage. For a short while she'd allowed herself to breathe freely again, to buy a paper in the local shop without worrying about who she might bump into. But now Lorna had returned and without her husband by her side, she was more of a threat than ever.

At first Lorna moved back to Great Shefford and it wasn't long before everyone knew that she and Paul had started their affair back up right where they'd left off. Small villages – even picturesque aga-saga ones such as this one – are a hotbed for gossip. Soon neighbours were once again looking at Rena with pity in their eyes.

'That poor woman,' they'd whisper. 'Right under her nose, too.'

Rena hated the well-intentioned pity, just as she'd loathed it when she was a neglected child. She didn't want sympathy; she wanted her marriage back. She'd put everything into that man and now he was throwing it all back in her face.

But Paul did little to reassure his distraught wife. By that stage he'd decided his marriage was well and truly over. He no longer cared about Rena or about what she might feel. He and Lorna seemed to go out of their way to rub her nose in it, once leaving empty champagne bottles and massage oil stains in the marital bed of the Salmons' holiday home in Dorset. Paul reckoned she would just have to get used to it. They were finished and that was that. Now it was only a question of sorting out the details, the finances and the divorce.

Any mention of the 'd' word sent Rena into a complete tailspin. She couldn't, *wouldn't* accept it. This was her man, her life. What gave this woman the right to steal it out from under her? Things had been all right until she came along. It wasn't fair!

Rena's behaviour became increasingly erratic. Paul would come home to find her drunk and barely coherent. One time, after she'd been drinking and taking morphine tablets, she climbed into her car and said she was going to kill herself. He followed in his own car – according to him to take her home again and according to her to make sure she went through with it. On another occasion, he claimed she'd texted her children while they were with him in the car to say that she was going to die and she'd see them in heaven. Instead, she woke up in hospital.

At the same time as her emotional state was spiralling out of control, Rena was trying to hang onto any last vestiges of ordinary family life that would help ground her in normality. While Paul was openly seeing her former friend, Rena would stay in the family home, lovingly washing and ironing his clothes. She still clung to the notion he'd change his mind and come back to her. Other times, though, the reality of the situation would consume her and she'd be filled with a fierce, uncontrollable rage.

One day Paul was at the family home when he got a call from a clearly frightened Lorna.

'Paul, Rena is here,' she told him.

In the background he could hear his wife banging on the door and shouting abuse. Somehow she then managed to gain entry. The next thing he heard was the sound of Lorna crying out as Rena attacked her.

Rushing over to Lorna's house, he saw his lover's Saab outside with the word 'whore' scrawled down the side and a neighbour standing between the two women, clearly trying to keep them apart. Lorna was holding her head while Rena, still beside herself with anger, continued to hurl a tirade of abuse at her. Finally managing to bundle his wife into the garden, Paul promised her he'd be home by 8.30pm and they'd talk then. By this stage he'd have said anything just to get her to leave. But when he didn't show up at the appointed time, Rena's rage was re-ignited. Dragging her two children out of bed in their pyjamas, she drove back over to Lorna's house.

'Now you can see what sort of a man your father is!' she yelled at the terrified children as she attacked Paul with a bunch of keys. The police were called.

Hell hath no fury like a woman scorned goes the old saying. Never has that been truer than in the case of Rena Salmon. Anger ate through her very being like acid. It was clear that Great Shefford was no longer big enough to contain the love-triangle threesome. In June 2002 Paul moved out of the family house and he and Lorna set up home in an apartment in Iver, Buckinghamshire. Finally they could be together shielded from Rena's volatile and increasingly unpredictable behaviour. Lorna stopped calling herself Rodrigues and reverted to her maiden name of Stewart. For the new lovers life seemed to be getting back on course.

But for Rena, left alone in the house she once thought would be the setting of a new life for herself and her husband, there would be no getting over it. Day after day she paced the rooms, each one alive with memories of Paul and of happier times. She found it hard to concentrate on anything; some days she even found it hard to breathe. Every waking moment was consumed with thoughts of Paul and Lorna together living the life that was rightfully hers. She just couldn't come to terms with it, any of it. Paul had vowed to love and cherish her as long as they both should live – not cast her off like last year's fashion mistake. It couldn't be real that he'd left her, that he was starting a life with someone else. There had to be a mistake.

If she could just find that one right thing to say, she was sure she could make him change his mind. He'd loved her once, he could love her again – all she had to do was make him see that she was still the same girl she'd been when he'd asked her to marry him all those years ago; but how?

Whenever Paul brought up the question of divorce, Rena's insides turned to jelly. She didn't want to talk about it, didn't want to face it. If she gave him a divorce, he'd marry Lorna and then there'd be another woman calling herself Mrs Salmon. Her role in life, the one she'd worked so hard for, would be stolen from her. Then who would she be? Back to being no one. There would be no divorce she insisted; just a separation.

But her mind wouldn't stop whirring. What if they had children? Lorna was only 36. It was quite possible. The very thought of it turned her stomach. She was the mother of Paul's children. No one else had the right to that title and certainly not that backstabbing bitch who used to call herself a friend.

Rena called Paul. 'I'll give you a divorce,' she apparently told him. 'But only if you have a vasectomy. I don't want lots of half bastards running around!' Paul's estranged wife was becoming increasingly unhinged. She promised her children not to make any more suicide attempts but one day she sat them down.

'I don't want to be alive any more,' she told them. 'I'm so sorry.'

The children, then aged 10 and 13, indicated they didn't want to be left behind and so Rena made a bizarre suicide pact with them. 'We'll have a great holiday and then I'll make hot chocolate laced with morphine, and we'll lie on my bed and I'll tell you stories until we all go to sleep,' she said. Luckily, in her current state of mind plans made one day were sure to be ditched the next and the suicide pact never came to pass but it's a chilling sign of how extreme her thoughts were getting.

Again and again Rena threatened to do harm to Lorna. Having been trained to use firearms in the army, most of her plans involved shooting the other woman. Paul, an avid hunter, owned three guns that he kept in the house in a locked cabinet.

'I don't want to kill her,' she told friend Leone Griffin. 'Just shoot her so that she can't have sex with him.' She bombarded Lorna Stewart with so many death threats on her mobile that she had to change her phone.

No one who knew her took her seriously. They assumed the threats were just a way of venting her anger. And really, they could see why she'd be enraged. Sometimes the things Lorna did and said verged on the cruel. Like when Rena asked her why she was having an affair with her husband and why she'd lied about finishing it. She supposedly replied: 'Because I can. Because you're fat, ugly and boring!'

Paul too seemed to get some kind of pleasure out of taunting his wife. She told friends that one time he'd texted her to say he couldn't make it back to visit the children because he was 'too busy shagging'.

One night Lorna called Rena to tell her that she and Paul were trying for a baby. According to Rena, she'd added: 'And it'll look just like us.' Of course the implication was that she and Paul would have a blue-eyed, fair-skinned baby unlike Rena herself or her children, who'd inherited her darker colouring. For Rena, whose own mother had made her feel second class because of her colour, this was the lowest of all blows. Again she was being made to feel worthless because of the colour of her skin – and worse, her children were also being targeted.

Her hatred for Lorna became like a once caged tiger that has escaped and now cannot be contained. Thoughts of vengeance on the other woman were never far from her mind. Her feelings for Paul, however, were more ambiguous. One minute she hated him for what he'd done to her and the next she remembered how much she loved and adored him. Her emotions were like a pendulum swinging relentlessly back and forth through her battered brain.

One morning in early September 2002 Paul Salmon received a card from his wife. Expecting a stream of vitriol, he was surprised by the gentle, reflective and even reasonable tone of the message inside.

'I wish I could go back to unspoiled times before hurt touched our hearts,' she wrote. 'If I could start from those moments once more, I'd hold you and tell you what you mean to me. I love you as I did then and always will.

'It's time for us to move on, but I want us to be friends for the kids.'

For the first time Paul dared to believe there might actually be some hope of an amicable divorce at least for the children's sake. Finally it sounded as if Rena was coming to terms with what had happened and realising she had no choice but to accept it.

By the next day, however, the pendulum had swung back and once again Rena was full of rage. Picking up the phone, Paul claims to have heard his wife once again threaten to kill Lorna.

'You'll never see your children again!' she yelled.

Shortly afterwards Rena Salmon phoned a nearby locksmith.

'My husband has been killed in a car accident,' she explained. 'We're separated and all the insurance policies are locked up in his weapons cabinet and the keys have gone missing. They were with him when he died.'

Sympathetic, the locksmith agreed to open the cabinet. Of course he had no idea that there was no dead husband, no insurance policy. What Rena wanted was the double-barrelled Beretta she'd bought Paul for his birthday.

Rena knew all about guns. During her time in the army she'd got used to handling them, used to the weight of them and the way they made your body jolt as you pulled the trigger. For her, guns held no fear, no mystery. They were simply a means to an end. For the next few days, Rena Salmon hugged her secret close to her chest. Knowing the cabinet was open and that she had access to weapons any time she chose gave her a sense of security and purpose lacking in the last few roller-coaster months.

No one can be really sure what she was planning to do with her new power. Was she intending to use the weapon on herself, knowing she surely wouldn't fail this way to finish the task she'd already tried? Or was Paul the intended victim; did she lie awake at night imagining how he'd look as he pleaded for his life, finally sorry for what he'd done, for what he'd driven her to?

Three days after the locksmith opened up Paul's gun cabinet, Rena bumped into her friend Deborah Burke. Deborah was saddened to see how the trauma of her husband's affair and the ensuing bitter marriage break-up had affected the once smiley woman.

'I know you're having a rough time,' Deborah comforted her.

Everyone in the neighbourhood knew Rena was going through hell. Locally, there was a lot of sympathy for the mother-of-two who'd invested so heavily in her marriage only to watch it blow up in her face. No wonder she was acting so strangely, people said. You couldn't blame her if she sometimes said or did things that seemed completely out of character. So when Rena told her friend: 'I have a gun,' Deborah Burke didn't take her too seriously. 'I'm not going to kill her –just shoot her here' (Rena indicated her abdomen) 'so she can't have any more babies.' It was the kind of crazy thing people say when they're out of their minds with grief and anger. 'You're going to get through this,' Deborah reassured her. 'You're tough.' But Rena didn't seem to be listening. 'If you see anything in the papers, it'll be me,' she said. Deborah laughed. 'Well, hell hath no fury like a woman scorned.' She could have had no idea how soon those words would come back to haunt her.

Not everyone was taking Rena's threats so lightly. Leone Griffin knew Rena had access to the gun cabinet and had talked to her husband Kevin about her concerns. Normally she wouldn't have thought too much of it – after all Paul had always had firearms around the house, but Rena had been so unstable recently, talking about killing herself and even her children, as well as Lorna. Leone was worried the open gun case would prove too much of a temptation.

Kevin rang Paul, expecting him to be horrified, but he was astounded when the other man calmly told him: 'I'm having dinner at the moment – I'll sort it later.' It seemed incredible. Here was a man being told his suicidal wife now had access to a gun and he seemed more concerned about finishing his dinner! Still, Paul knew his wife better than anyone. Maybe he knew these threats of Rena's weren't really serious. Who knows? Perhaps Rena had said this sort of things before and never acted on it. As everyone always says, you never really know what goes on behind closed doors in someone else's relationship.

And so, in a quaint little English village where by rights Women's Institute members should be meeting to discuss fundraising cake sales and rivalry limited to competition between different brownie groups, guns, suicide and murder were the subjects on people's lips. Still, no one really believed anything would happen. This wasn't Downtown LA or Hackney's Murder Mile: this was Great Shefford, where every other house boasted a conservatory and people still attended church on Sundays.

On 10 September, the day before Paul and Rena Salmon were due in court for a divorce hearing Rena woke up feeling like a rubber band stretched so far that it was at breaking point. Today something had to give; she didn't think she could take any more.

There are days when you feel you've literally reached your limit. Sure, your rational self tells you that if you can just get through this one day, this one night, everything will work itself out somehow. Yet, to the other part of yourself where emotions run as thickly as blood, one day or night more seems unthinkable.

While her daughter was getting ready for school, Rena loaded the shotgun into her Mercedes. In her version of events, she was planning to drive to Lorna's salon in Chiswick and shoot herself in front of her, hoping a death on the premises would cause her rival's business to nosedive. The version put forward by the prosecution in her trial asserted that it was always Lorna and not herself that was the target. In either case it's a scenario almost too chilling to imagine. The new school year has just started. Uniforms are still virtually pristine, smart new pens nestle in virgin pencil cases. A loving mother drops her 10-year-old daughter at the school gates knowing that the boot of the car holds a shotgun and that at the end of the school day, someone will be dead and Mummy won't be coming home.

In those circumstances how do you say goodbye? Do you dwell on a face, trying to memorise each beloved feature? Or is the adrenaline rush too strong and too urgent to allow space for emotions? Does the need to get going and do what must be done overpower the maternal urge to linger and caress? If a woman – even fleetingly – allows herself to think like a mother, can she really go ahead and do what Rena Salmon did?

Chiswick in west London is conveniently placed for easy access from Berkshire. That was one of the reasons why Lorna Stewart had been able to successfully combine running a beauty salon with being a mother. It didn't take Rena long to drive the 60 miles there and find a parking space. Getting out of her car, she casually reached into the boot and pulled out the shotgun. Walking calmly past an electrician working on the salon – a respectable, relaxed-looking 40-something woman who just happened to be carrying a shotgun – she barely merited a raised eyebrow. Obviously there had to be a good reason for the gun, he reasoned, perhaps it was a fake or an amateur dramatics prop.

'Don't shoot!' he joked, raising his hands in mock terror.

If only Rena Salmon had heeded that advice.

Instead she made her way down the salon stairs. Lorna

Stewart was in the office with her bookkeeper Lindsey Rees. The two were chatting together as they went about the normal day-to-day chores that running a business entails. Lindsey was writing a cheque while Lorna – with her back to her – crouched on the floor looking through papers. It was a typical, slow weekday and the two women had no reason to suppose anything out of the ordinary was going to happen.

Hunched over the chequebook, Lindsey heard Lorna say 'Hello Rena' in an unemotional tone. She could have been greeting the mailman or a familiar client. Glancing up, Lindsey saw someone in the doorway. Then Lorna spoke again, using the same calm almost monotone voice.

'So you have come to shoot me?'

The reply came back in the same chillingly calm, controlled manner.

'Yes.'

Would things have happened differently if Lorna had used a different greeting? If she hadn't put the idea of murder out there so it danced tantalisingly in the air between them. Was it suggestion, invitation or statement of fact?

'What about the children?' Lorna asked.

Rena was momentarily thrown. 'What about *your* children? You have left them in Australia,' she said, uncomprehending. It was left to Lorna to explain as if Rena herself was a child.

'What about *your* children?' she asked.

If this was a plea for her life, a desperate attempt to get Rena to reconsider, Lorna Stewart was certainly being very cool about it. Faced with the woman who'd threatened her life on numerous occasions and now stood in front of her holding a loaded gun, she never raised her voice, never became hysterical. And Rena seemed to follow her cue, remaining unnaturally calm, completely focused on Lorna, never looking anywhere else.

'They will be looked after by Paul,' she replied.

Then, as if there was nothing more to say, Rena fired the gun.

As Lorna toppled over and fell to the floor, Lindsey Rees jumped to her feet and ran out of the office and up the stairs. As she reached the top, she heard another shot.

Downstairs Rena Salmon walked calmly over to Lorna and took her by the hand. She maintains Lorna was still alive at this point and, as she squeezed her hand, they reverted to the close friends they'd once been – two best friends facing death together.

Rena reached for her phone and dialled 999, telling the operator: 'I've just shot my husband's mistress.'

'Do you want to give yourself up?' she was asked.

'Yeah,' came the reply. 'I'm sitting with her.'

When the operator asked the caller's name, there was the same unhurried and almost casual air about her reply: 'Rena Salmon – Salmon as in the fish. Right, got to go.'

After that, Rena smoked first one cigarette and then a

second as she sat next to Lorna Stewart's now motionless body. While she waited, she sent a series of text messages.

'I've shot Lorna, you pushed me to it,' read the one she sent to husband Paul.

Then she sent a message to Leone Griffin: 'I've shot Lorna. Look after my daughter for me.'

At first Leone couldn't take it seriously.

'I hope it's a joke,' she messaged back.

When she got no reply, Leone rang Rena. 'What have you done?' she demanded. 'I hope you're joking.'

But this was no joke. In the same calm voice, Rena said, 'No, I've shot her. Once in the back and once in the side, and she's lying on the floor.'

By this time Paul Salmon had received the harrowing text from his wife and was on his way to the salon. He rang Rena from his car.

'What have you done?' he yelled.

'I've shot Lorna,' Rena repeated.

'Is she dead?' Paul demanded, trying to keep control of his emotions as he drove to the scene.

'I don't know,' came the answer.

There's nothing more surreal than being in a familiar place where something cataclysmic has taken place. All the physical surroundings are the same – the grey streets, with the odd bit of litter blowing in the gutter, the same shop fronts, the same peeling posters, and yet something fundamental has shifted so it's as if you are seeing it all for the first time. Everything is different and nothing will ever be quite the same again.

Paul Salmon pulled up in front of the salon on 10 September with his heart pounding. It was as if he was in a film, as if it was all happening to someone else. Unfortunately, this was one movie he couldn't pause or switch off, or walk out of. By the time he arrived, the police were already there: Lorna Stewart was dead and it was all over; it was all too late.

★ ★ ★ ★ ★

After a 9-day trial in which her defence team sought to prove that she was a devoted wife who was traumatised by an unhappy childhood and pushed to the brink of insanity by a cruel and unfaithful husband, on 16 May 2003 Rena Salmon was found guilty of murder and sentenced to life imprisonment. The court was then told that Lorna had been two months' pregnant at the time she was killed. Rena's worst fears had been on course, after all.

In the fallout from one violent death, many lives can be radically altered. Paul Salmon, who went on record saying he had 'no regrets' about his affair with love-of-his-life Lorna and no guilt about cheating on Rena, was divorced a month after the trial ended. Six months later he was engaged to his new girlfriend.

Both the Salmon and the Rodrigues children are

growing up without a mother and Keith Rodrigues, who never stopped loving his wife, knows there'll always be an empty space at special family occasions no one else can fill.

As for Rena Salmon herself, faced with a lifetime of imprisonment she has had all the time in the world to think about what she did and all the time in the world for regrets. She knows she will miss her children growing up; she'll miss being there when they rip open their exam results and miss waving them off on their first day of university. She won't be there to wipe their tears when they experience the first heartbreak of young love, nor will she share their everyday fears and frustrations, their disappointments and their triumphs.

Rena has told friends that Lorna haunts her and she would do anything to swap places with her. She may be eligible for parole in 2017, but even then she will take her past with her: things that are done can never be undone.

When a marriage breaks down in bitterness there are no winners and when the fetid entrails of a life together are spilled out on the pavement for all the world to see there can be only losers.

It's something Rena Salmon knows only too well.

CHAPTER TWO

THE DENTIST
OF DEATH

When Kelly Comeau's doorbell went at an hour verging on the uncivilised one Saturday morning early in December 2004, she was mildly irritated but not unduly alarmed. Bogan Gates Drive in the Sugar Hill district of Buford, Georgia, is the sort of leafy, upper-middle class street where an early knock on the door on a weekend morning in December most likely heralds the arrival of the postman carrying an extra-large, early Christmas present. Or it might be an over-zealous charity collector trying to catch folk's Christmas spirit before wallet-fatigue sets in.

City folk from downtown Atlanta disdainfully refer to Sugar Hill and its neighbouring suburbs as OTP – Outside the Perimeter – but by and large its residents believe they are well and truly living the American Dream. With its spacious, attractive houses, neatly planted gardens, golf courses and friendly local schools, it's the white picket fence version of Modern American life. Children tear round the quiet streets on bikes or play Little League baseball in the park while their mothers bake cakes for church fundraisers or sit on neighbourhood committees. It's the kind of place where couples present a smiling united front to the world while their marriages unravel secretly and privately behind firmly closed doors. As you cross the Dekalb/Gwinnett City Line on your way to the Sugar Hill area the sign on the Water Tower reads 'Success Lives Here' and with success in residence, anything less just isn't tolerated. Among the shiny, polished-on-Sundays estate cars and living rooms adorned with poster-sized, studio-posed family photos there's no place for self-doubt, failure or dysfunction.

Yet that Saturday morning something new and uninvited moved into Bogan Gates Drive, something pervasive and unpleasant that no quantity of disinfectant wipes or collective prayers at Sunday service could ever cleanse or dislodge. Evil came snaking in down the quiet suburban street, into houses with the curtains still drawn against the early morning light, up wide carpeted staircases and along hallways lined with framed homilies and family snapshots. Evil came calling and nothing there would ever be the same again.

Standing on the Comeau's doorstep at 7.40am that Saturday morning, 4 December, was little Dalton Corbin, one of the two boys who lived across the street. Neighbours for the past few years, the Comeaus and the Corbins were extremely close and forever in and out of one another's houses. They shared babysitting, dinner and barbecues. The Comeaus had even willed their estate and care of their child to the Corbins in the event of their death. While the Corbins' relationship had recently been going through a rocky patch, Bart Corbin, the boys' dad, spent at lot of time at the Comeaus' house to escape for a while the tensions of home. That's how close the two families were. But young Dalton Corbin's early morning visit, this cold December morning, was far from a normal social call.

Wearing just his underpants, the 7-year- old was shivering in the biting winter wind and gulping back hysterical tears. What he had to say would shatter the peace of that quiet neighbourhood for years to come and destroy the lives of two families:

'My Dad shot my Mom.'

★ ★ ★ ★ ★

On the surface of things, the Corbins looked as if they had it all. Mum, Jennifer, was a tall, attractive blonde with a smile that came right from the soul. A pre-school teacher at the church, she was heavily involved in the local community and devoted a large chunk of her boundless energy to helping on neighbourhood committees and organising children's sporting teams. She was just one of those rare people who love to give. You know how some people commit selfless acts for selfish reasons – to look good or because they think it's what they're supposed to do? Well, Jennifer Barber-Corbin wasn't like that. Whether it was time, money or love, she gave because it was what came naturally and it would never have occurred to her to do anything else. Her sister, Heather Tierney, recalls supermarket shopping with Jennifer and being baffled when she bought a pre-baked chicken, then left it behind at the check out desk. It turned out Jennifer – or Jenn as she was known to her many friends – had spotted a local homeless man in the shop and had bought the chicken for him, making sure the cashier would quietly hand it to him as he left. That was the kind of person she was.

While Jenn Corbin cared about everyone around her, when it came to her immediate family, her generosity and capacity for love knew no bounds. She showered her two small sons – Dalton, and his 5-year-old brother Dillon – with affection, inventing games for them, turning ordinary moments into adventures. The boys were her work in progress and to this deeply religious woman they were her gift from God. Dalton was bright, outgoing and inquisitive while Dillon was dreamier and quieter yet both represented her investment in the future, the embodiment of her dreams and hopes.

Family was immensely important to Jenn. She and her two sisters, Heather and Rajel Caldwell, had grown up in a home where money was sometimes tight but love was limitless. Their parents, Max and Narda Barber, were so close to their offspring that even as adults the girls couldn't bear to move far from one another or from their mum and dad. Each birthday or anniversary was an excuse for a family get together and the whole clan enjoyed holidays together, boating on Lake Lanier.

Back in the early nineties when Jenn first introduced new boyfriend Barton (Bart) Corbin to her family the Barbers immediately welcomed him. She'd met him through his younger brother Robert – who was working for the same seafood chain of restaurants – and was instantly drawn to him, as were her family. 'He cracks me up,' Heather told Jenn approvingly. 'He's so funny.' And with his dark hair, chiselled features and piercing brown eyes, Bart was no slouch in the looks department either. His self-contained dry wit was a perfect counterbalance to Jenn's larger-than life exuberance and zest for living.

Jenn was never very materialistic but it didn't hurt that as an up-and-coming dentist with a burgeoning practice in nearby Dacula and a fiercely ambitious streak, Bart Corbin would also be able to provide handsomely for her and any children they might have. For the Barber family, Bart

Corbin seemed a great choice for their precious Jenn. Sure, he might use more colourful language than Max and Narda were used to but he slotted right into the family and in no time at all was sharing weekends with Jenn's sisters and holidays with the whole clan. When the couple married in September 1996 in a beautiful garden ceremony, everyone agreed it was one of the most uplifting weddings they'd ever witnessed. Later, when Dalton and Dillon came along, two years apart, Barton's place in the family was well and truly secured. Sometimes when Max and Narda looked around at their kids and grandkids in the middle of a family gathering they felt a huge swell of pride. Not only had their daughters turned into such fine people but they'd introduced equally interesting and decent partners into the family mix, too. How lucky they were!

What the Barbers didn't know was that their perfect new son-in-law was carrying round a terrible secret, a secret that had the power to blow their whole happy family world to pieces. If Max and Narda had realised what dark shadows lurked in Bart Corbin's past, they would have scooped up their big-hearted Jenn, size 9½ feet and all, and her two tousle-haired boys and run to the farthest corner of the earth. If they'd seen past Bart's pleasant, respectable exterior to the depths of his contorted soul, they'd never have let Jenn go home to 4515 Bogan Gates Drive, where she would close the curtains against the night and double lock the front door thinking she was keeping the bad things away. Sometimes, just sometimes, the stranger you should most fear turns out to be the person you know best.

So when did it all start to fragment, this perfect all-American family life? When did the first cracks begin to thread their snake-like way across the fragile glass surface of the bright, shiny Barber-Corbin façade? Could anyone have spotted the early warning signs? Might they have prevented what happened from occurring? That's the problem with death, isn't it? It sentences those left behind to a lifetime of 'should haves' and 'what ifs'.

Throughout 2004 there was a gradual build up of tension in the house on Bogan Gates Drive. Bart, who'd always had a strong controlling streak, started to lose his temper more readily with Jenn and the boys. His work kept him away for long periods of time and, unbeknown to anyone else, he had become embroiled in a long-term affair. All Jenn knew was that even when he was home Bart seemed distant. It seemed that nothing she did was good enough any more; nothing made him happy.

Increasingly isolated and depressed, Jenn started to look for distraction on the internet, staying up long into the night after her children had gone to sleep and exchanging jokes with strangers in chat rooms or playing the hugely popular online role-playing game EverQuest. Sometimes she'd switch on her computer and lose herself so completely in the fantasy game – which involves teams of four players working together on various missions – that she'd suddenly realise with a jolt that hours had passed since she'd first sat down. Still, at least it kept her mind busy and stopped her from thinking too much about how unhappy she was becoming in her marriage.

For Jenn, part of the enjoyment of online game playing was 'meeting' so many new people. To the uninitiated, online gaming can seem like a solitary pursuit but for many players it provides access to a ready-made support group, an instant community of like-minded 'friends'. So what if you never get to meet them in person? For many, hiding behind usernames and pseudonyms is a kind of release. You're free to reinvent yourself, to become the person you always dreamed of being. For Jennifer Corbin, devoted mother of two, volunteer at the local church, wife of a successful, well-respected dentist, the anonymity afforded by the internet meant that for once she no longer had to pretend to be living an enviable perfect life with the perfect husband. For a few hours a day she got to shake off the dual shackles of keeping up appearances and of living up to other people's expectations; she was free to be herself.

Sometime over the course of 2004 Jenn struck up a conversation online with someone called Christopher. Although they knew nothing about one another, there seemed to be an instant connection between them. Christopher got her sense of humour and he was interested in the same things. Before long, the two were chatting as if they'd known each other all their lives and Jenn was sharing some of her frustrations about the state of her marriage. Although she had plenty of friends locally, Christopher was different. He was far enough removed from her everyday life that she didn't feel like she was being judged and was consequently more able to talk freely. Not only this but he also had an uncanny ability to instinctively understand how she was feeling. Before long the online friendship had strengthened into something much deeper and the two were exchanging increasingly intimate and romantic messages. For Jenn it was like a new beginning – a lifeline in the increasingly stormy waters of her marriage.

Then Christopher dropped a bombshell. It seemed he was not who he said he was. In fact, he was not even a 'he'. Christopher turned out to be Anita, a Missouri woman, who'd also turned to the internet in a search for comfort and in the hope of finding a soulmate. At first Jenn was heartbroken. Just when she thought she'd found someone special, someone who understood her, who supported her when everything looked so hopeless, it was all snatched away from her. In an increasingly bleak situation this had been her one ray of happiness and now it had gone. Was she destined to feel lonely all her life?

As the shock waves began to ebb away and Jenn had time to absorb what had happened, she began to reconsider her earlier outrage. Did it really make a difference who or what 'Christopher' was if 'he' made her feel good? If you were lucky enough to find a soulmate, shouldn't you hang onto them no matter what? Soon Jenn and 'Christopher' were exchanging emails again and before long, they'd started talking on the phone – warm, involved conversations that often went on into the night.

'All she's done is show me that I don't have to be unhappy for the rest of my life,' explained Jenn to her sister, Heather. 'Don't I deserve that?' But no one could have begrudged Jenn, who always put herself out so much for everyone else, this chance of companionship with someone who cared.

If you've ever lain awake at night beside someone you no longer love while resentment lies in between you like a third person or if you've ever stayed up late in the hope that your partner would be asleep by the time you got to bed, or gone up early feigning a headache; if you've ever leaned against the closed door of the en suite bathroom running the tap to cover the sound of your wretchedness, you'll know something of what Jennifer Barber-Corbin went through those last few months of her life. Look into your heart. Imagine being in that cold place gazing at a turned back, searching the silences for hidden meanings. Could you blame her for seeking out friendship wherever she could find it, for turning towards the warmth of someone who understands?

Perhaps it was the strength she gathered from her new companion that helped Jenn to resolve finally to bring an end to her increasingly unhappy marriage. 'Mom, I do not love Bart,' she told her worried mother, Narda. 'I have loved him because he is the father of our children but I'm ready to leave and I'm ready to get on with my life.' No parent ever wants to hear that their child is thinking of divorce and particularly when they've taken their son-in-law into their family and their heart. Narda and Max Barber knew their daughter, however, and they were certain she wouldn't have given up on her marriage without having exhausted every option for staying together. Besides they'd also grown slightly alarmed at the way Bart sometimes snapped at Jenn or the boys. He seemed to want to orchestrate everything they did and grew irrationally irritated if they deviated from his plans.

All the family had witnessed Bart losing his temper with Jenn or the boys. Heather had been horrified when Dalton had struck out at a Little League baseball game and Bart had yelled at him from the stands, calling him an idiot and a loser. It was hardly a bolt from the blue to hear that Jenn had had enough. But over the autumn of 2004, as the humid heat of the Georgia summer gave way to cooler, fresher days, Jenn's attention was increasingly distracted – not only by the computer but also the demands of two active young sons, a large home and a full social calendar. Meanwhile her husband was growing more watchful and more thoughtful.

Bart Corbin was a man used to being in control. After an unremarkable childhood in Snellville, Georgia, where his father was a military policeman and his mother a bank teller, his life so far had followed the path he'd always intended – good job, attractive wife, sporty kids. He could move around the area in which he lived knowing that people were looking at him with admiration and even envy. He had the plush office, the beautiful brick house; he was a man of standing, a man to be reckoned with. Divorce didn't feature anywhere in his carefully constructed view of himself. A public marriage break-up would mean a drastic change in his standard of living. He would probably lose his home and he would miss out on precious moments with his sons but more than that he would have to admit failure into his life. His perfect existence would turn out to be flawed just like everyone else's. No longer would people look at him as a man who has everything, no longer would he command total respect. His grand design would be thwarted and he would be just like anyone else. And it would be all Jenn's fault.

Where do you start to chart the timeline of the disintegration of a marriage? Is it the first argument or the first doubts? Maybe it's the first time he forgets her birthday or she falls asleep without curling into his back. In the end it doesn't matter where the rot starts, what matters is how it finishes. And once the unravelling begins, the finish comes all too quickly.

Thanksgiving 2004 was an uncharacteristically tense affair for the Barber family. As usual the whole clan were gathered together – this year at Heather's house in nearby Dawsonville, with its motley zoo of pet animals and fenced-in back yard with the grass worn bald in the places where the kids particularly liked to play. Although the family enjoyed spending time together and watching all the small cousins racing around and stuffing themselves with food when they thought no one else was looking as usual, there was an edge to the atmosphere as never before.

Usually urbane and convivial at these occasions, Bart seemed ill at ease and withdrawn. Unusually, he spent much of the day on his own, out on the porch or in the basement. When he did join the family, he was sombre and out of sorts. At 6pm he got to his feet and announced his family was leaving. 'Aw, no!' protested the boys. 'Why do we have to go so early?' But Jenn knew better than to antagonise her husband. She told the boys that if their father was determined to leave, they'd better start getting ready to go. The others tried to talk them into staying. Family occasions just weren't the same without everyone there. Besides there was something about Bart's manner, something about the tight set of his mouth and the suppressed anger in his eyes that concerned them. They'd all witnessed Bart's displays of temper and wanted to keep Jenn and her kids safely with them.

But Jenn knew her husband and she understood that the longer she delayed leaving, the angrier he would get. Better to get it over with now then at least her family would be free to enjoy the rest of their day without the constant undercurrent of friction. Besides, maybe it would all blow over. Perhaps it was one of Bart's sudden mood swings that would be forgotten by the time they got home. Unfortunately this was one mood that wasn't going to go quite so quickly. You see, the ever-wary Barton Corbin had decided it was time he started to look into exactly what his wife was doing all those long hours spent online with her long, capable fingers tap-tapping over the keyboard, her unruly blonde hair pushed behind her ears. What he discovered incensed him beyond reason. Not only had his wife developed an intense and intimate friendship with a stranger online but she was also divulging details of their marriage. For the privacy-loving dentist, this was the grossest betrayal.

There are some occasions where you know before you even get into the car that this is going to be a nightmare journey. Those are the times when you drag out the goodbyes at the kerbside or linger while filling up the boot of the car with children's toys and empty dishes long since cleared of the food you lovingly prepared for the family feast. These are the times when you fuss unnecessarily about strapping your protesting children into the back seat and take a deep breath before opening up the passenger door. The times when you prepare yourself for the blast of barely repressed anger that hits you like a sledgehammer before you've even sat down. And the drive home from Heather's house was such an occasion.

Barton Corbin was fuming. All day long he'd allowed his rage and resentment to build up, stifling it behind a façade of family togetherness and idle chat. All day he'd watched his wife laughing and joking with her sisters, heaping praise on the food, goofing around with the children without betraying a hint of her double life. Oh, she gave a very good impression of being such a perfect wife and mother. What would her family think if they knew how she was opening up their private life to strangers on the net? Or maybe they were already in on it; maybe she'd already whinged to them about how miserable she was in her marriage and how she was planning to leave her nasty old husband. The same husband who bought her a beautiful house in the best neighbourhood and made sure she had enough for nice clothes and fun vacations. Oh yes, Barton was mad all right. He'd worked his behind off for this woman and this was how she repaid him – by forming inappropriate relationships online and spilling the secrets of their private life to strangers. Well, she had another thing coming if she thought he was just going to lie down and accept it. No one ever called Barton Corbin a pushover.

As soon as Jenn got in the car, he started on her. Who was this person she'd been sending so many emails to? She was a slut, Barton yelled. 'Not in front of the children,' Jennifer pleaded. 'We can talk about this at home.' But Barton had had all day to stew and he wasn't about to start being reasonable now. They hadn't driven far before things

47

got very heated within the cramped confines of that car. Bart Corbin, the man who prided himself on his self-control, for once allowed his guard to drop and rage to take over. Who did she think she was, arguing with him? How *dare* she? Impulsively, he reached out and punched his wife in the face. Jenn gasped in disbelief, her hand flying up to touch her stinging cheek. 'I never touched you,' snarled the deranged dentist. 'It's your word against mine!'

The line had been crossed. From that point on there would be no going back. Never again would the Corbins appear to the outside world as the perfect family. She'd suspected it before, but now Jenn knew beyond all doubt that beneath her husband's charming, educated veneer lurked a sinister violent streak. He was not going to let her get away without a fight. But what she couldn't have known and would never have believed was that it would be a fight to the death – her own.

An hour after leaving her sister's house, Jenn was on the phone to Heather, recounting the sickening details of the scene in the car. Heather couldn't believe it. 'Come right back here,' she begged her sister. Not long after Heather picked up the phone to her distraught sister, her husband Doug's mobile rang. It was Bart, still seething and determined to put his side of the story across. 'Whatever she says, it's a lie!' he yelled, adding that Dalton was too young to testify. Meanwhile, Jenn was now on the phone to her father, who told her to grab her things, take the kids and get out of the house. Clearly alarmed by the violent turn the relationship had taken, Max even warned Jenn to take a different route back to Heather's house to make sure she couldn't be followed.

Within an hour Jenn and the boys were back on Heather's doorstep. Needing to be surrounded by people who loved her, she stayed the night. Her boys were clearly traumatised by the scene they'd witnessed in the car and Dalton refused to leave his mother's side even to sleep. By now there was no disguising the fact that this was a marriage in meltdown. 'You have to leave him, Jenn,' urged her worried family. After all, if Barton Corbin was capable of punching his wife in the face in front of their children, how much worse might things get when they were on their own?

Alone in the family home, Barton had plenty of time to brood on the situation. So his wife wanted to leave him, did she? She'd soon discover that he wasn't someone to be messed with. Jennifer would get a big shock if she thought he was just going to waltz off quietly, leaving her to carry on her pathetic little internet 'relationships' while his sons were sleeping upstairs in his home. No, sir! This would not happen.

On the Friday after Thanksgiving, Barton was round for dinner at his friends and neighbours, giving the Comeaus his version of what had happened. Stuck awkwardly in the middle, Kelly and Steve did what any mutual friends do in this situation – they tried to give support, while remaining neutral. 'You'll be OK, Bart, after all this is over,' Kelly Comeau reassured him. But Barton was far from OK: he was furious. A man given to obsession, he kept going over and over the injustice of what had happened – and what was still happening. He had provided for his wife, he had given her two children and a great life and now she wanted to end the relationship, to throw him away like yesterday's newspaper. How ungrateful could you get? Well, he'd show her.

On 29 November 2004 Barton Corbin filed for divorce in Gwinnett County Superior Court. On his list of demands were the Bogan Gates Drive house, the furniture, his attorney fees, child support and custody of the boys. The battle lines were well and truly drawn.

There's truly no prison more terrifying, no situation more lonely or oppressive than a marital home where a couple is at war. Jennifer Corbin knew she had to go back to Bogan Gates Drive to maintain her legal rights over the house and to re-establish some degree of normality for her boys but doing so was like plunging into a waking nightmare. All that week she went about her daily business – taking the kids back and forth to basketball practice, cooking meals, buying the odd Christmas gift – but the whole time she had a shaky feeling in the pit of her stomach that things were going very, very wrong. Barton had moved out of their bedroom and into another part of the house, but his presence hung in the very air of that home like a dark, smothering cloud, leaking out droplets of bitterness and hatred.

Jennifer started to plan her escape, opening up a separate bank account and buying a secret mobile phone. In some ways it was exciting to think of starting over again with a clean slate and no more arguments but at the same time it was also terrifying. By this stage Jenn was 33, not old by any means but still a long way from the carefree art student she'd been when she first met Barton Corbin. It was daunting to think of being on her own again particularly when she felt so emotionally drained by the current situation.

As was her habit, Jenn confided many of these fears in her personal journal. This was her way of dealing with the internal conflicts and worries that she didn't want to burden other people with. Somehow just the act of getting them down on paper made her feel as if a weight had been taken off. Seeing her problems written out sometimes enabled her to look at them more clearly and even made them less threatening. Plus of course a journal was the ideal place to write about her most private thoughts and feelings, including those about her deepening online relationship so you can imagine how she felt when she walked into her room early in the morning on 1st December. She had just finished her early morning session on the treadmill downstairs when she found the contents of her handbag strewn over the floor and several items missing, including her new mobile phone and her journal. She knew beyond doubt that it was Barton who'd taken her things and she realised he'd try to use whatever he found in the journal against her if it came to a custody battle. She felt violated. How could he do something like that? How low would he go? She had to get her things back.

Furious, she rushed off to confront her husband. 'You give me my stuff back!' she demanded. Barton refused, and wearing only a towel wrapped round his waist, he fled from the house to the car and drove over Jenn's foot in his haste to get away. Sobbing, she dialled 911 to file a criminal complaint against her husband. 'He's probably gonna take them and use them as evidence against me,' she told the operator she said as she reported the theft of her things. 'We're in the process of going through a divorce.'

When the police arrived she was still distraught and reluctant to go back into the house but the attending officers could see no compelling reason to arrest the well-respected dentist. After all, people do a lot of crazy things in the heat of a marriage break-up. If they went round arresting every divorcing man who had a vicious row with his wife, they'd never have time for anything else. But Jenn was shaken to the core. She had known that Barton wouldn't give her up without a struggle but now she was beginning to get some idea of the lengths to which he was prepared to go to get what he wanted – or, perhaps more accurately, to make damn sure she didn't get what she wanted.

It's scary, isn't it, how quickly love can turn to hate; how the person you once cared the most for can so rapidly become the person to whom you wish most harm? The sad truth is that lovers make the worst enemies and Jenn Corbin was gradually realising this. For the sake of the two boys, she maintained the façade of everyday life although she wasn't able to shield them from the worst of the fighting but inside her heart felt like it was slowly constricting. How on earth were they going to get through Christmas? Every day she spoke to her parents and sister to let them know she was OK and to talk a bit about what was going on. Now they all knew Barton was capable of violence, but Jenn counted on the fact that with a divorce pending he wasn't going to do anything to jeopardise his chances of getting what he wanted.

During one phone call she confessed to Heather that even her children had started to fear for her. 'Dalton is saying he's afraid Bart is going to kill me,' she admitted. Heather was horrified: 'Jennifer, do you think he will?' The answer was carefully thought out. 'I don't think he would because I don't think he'd do that to the kids.' Heather couldn't believe they were even discussing this subject, much less that her beloved big sister was actually rationalising why her own husband would refrain from killing her. 'Jennifer, that's a bad reason,' she told her.

And so the week passed. Who knew then that this would be the last week of Jennifer Corbin's life? As they passed her in the grocery store rushing to get on with their day, or gave her a quick wave at school pick-up time, who realised this could be the last chance they'd have to talk to this big-hearted woman? Or that so strong a life force could be extinguished so suddenly and so brutally?

On Friday, 3 December, Heather didn't get a call from Jenn. She thought about calling her herself, but if the truth be told she was exhausted. As a mother of two pre-school children, she was finding her sister's domestic traumas emotionally draining. She decided she couldn't face dealing with it all that day, that just for that one day, she'd take a day off. What harm could it do?

There are some decisions you take so lightly, but weigh so heavily. Now Jenn's friends and family are full of the 'if onlys' which are the deadliest legacy of a life rubbed out prematurely. If only they'd realised what Barton Corbin was capable of, if only they'd stopped to chat, if only they'd told Jenn to watch her back – to lock her door, to run, to get out. Because even then, while Jenn was shopping and doing school-runs, Barton was taking steps to get rid of his wife once and for all. He phoned an old friend – Richard Wilson – and told him that he was worried his wife was cheating on him and he might need a gun to protect himself. Wilson had just traded a used lawnmower for a revolver and now he offered it to his friend. After all, mates should look after each other, shouldn't they? On 30 November, the day before Jenn phoned 911 accusing her husband of taking her possessions, Bart went to visit Wilson at home in Troy, Alabama to pick up the .38 calibre Smith and Wesson.

Who knows what went through his mind between 30 November and 4 December 2004? Did he pick up the gun in his hands, turning it over and over, wondering whether he really had the nerve to go through with this? Did his mind wander back to the other time he'd held a similar gun – how it had felt, and how it had all ended up? Did he think about his boys left alone without a mother, or Jenn's mum losing a daughter? And what about the big hole he'd leave in the lives of everyone that knew and loved her? What goes through the mind of a killer before he gives himself permission to take a life? If we knew that then maybe we'd all have it within us to do what Barton Corbin did.

Just before 1.45am on Saturday 4 December, Steve Comeau was smoking a cigarette in his garage when he noticed Bart's Chevy pick-up pulling up outside his house across the street. Just twenty minutes later he was gone again. Something about the briefness of the visit at this late hour disturbed Steve. 'I hope he didn't do anything stupid,' he thought to himself, remembering the theft allegations of just a few days before. But what Barton Corbin had done went way beyond the worst things Steve Comeau could imagine.

The following morning Dalton Corbin stood shivering and crying in his underwear on the Comeau's doorstep. 'My Dad shot my Mom,' he said. Unable to take in what Dalton had said, Kelly Comeau ran over the road to her friends' house. It was a journey she'd made so many times before – taking over freshly baked cookies, carrying home sleeping children – but this time everything was different. In the main bedroom she found Jennifer, dressed in her night-gown and lying on her side in the bed. There was a single wound to her head, a trail of blood coming from her nose and a gun tucked under the sheet, close to her hands.

How do you deal with a situation like that? One of your closest friends lies lifeless and bloody just yards from your home, her children traumatised, her husband missing. How do you stop the rush of emotions – grief, panic, shock, pity, horror from leaving you rooted to the spot? Kelly Comeau knew she had to get out of there. Fast. Scooping up 5-year-old Dillon Corbin, who'd been left in the house when his older brother dashed across the street, she ran back to her house and headed straight for the phone to dial 911. 'My girlfriend's dead!' she gasped to the operator. 'She's been shot. Her son just ran over and got me.' When the operator asked whether the victim could be helped, Kelly's response was heartbreaking in its finality. 'No,' she whispered.

It was still early on a Saturday morning. Just a few miles away Jennifer's sister Heather Tierney was starting her weekend blissfully oblivious to the events unfolding in Bogan Gates Drive. Anyone who has ever lost someone close to them will know how time automatically slices itself down the middle, dividing itself into 'Life Before It Happened' and 'Life After'. Heather didn't know it then but that Saturday as she listened to the excited babble of her young children and opened the curtains on another new day she was enjoying the last few moments of Life Before.

How many times since has she tried to find her way back to those moments when the world was normal, when Jenn was alive and murder was something that happened on the news, something that happened to other people? Then came the phone call that would shatter her life like so many pieces of broken china. Sure, she would eventually glue it back together again for the sake of the children and her husband Doug but it would never be the same again.

'Something's happened to Jenn.' Strange how four words can make a world stop spinning, freezing it in time and space so that one moment becomes an eternity. 'Is she OK?' That glimmer of hope, of denial – how bad can it be? But then came the words that kill all hope dead: 'She's gone.' For Heather, who'd looked up to her big sister from birth, admired and adored her and gone on to become her best friend, it was too much to take in. She felt as if the air was literally being sucked out of her body; she fell to her knees, screaming. Trying to dress herself, she found she couldn't stop shaking. Away from her children, she screamed and stamped her feet, trying to make the nightmare stop. It was she who had to make the phone call to her mother – the call no sibling should ever have to make and no parent should have to receive. Hysterical, Narda in turn rang Max at the car dealer's where he worked, making him the next heartbroken link in this most tragic of chains. 'I just hung up the phone and I drove straight to the house,' Max recalled later. 'I pulled up in the driveway behind a couple of Gwinnett County police cruisers. They wouldn't let me see my daughter.' Instead he went across the street to the Comeaus, where his two traumatised grandsons sat uncomprehending, their small bodies wrapped in blankets. Dalton was sobbing uncontrollably while Dillon just gazed silently around him.

Dalton talked in a rush about what had happened, about the fights he'd witnessed, about finding his mother. Mercifully he hadn't seen what happened but in his 7-year-old mind he had no doubt about the true state of affairs: his Dad had shot his Mum. For the attending police officers, however, the case was less cut and dried. Here was a woman going through an incredibly bitter divorce. The divorce papers were found scattered on the bed, her hands over the gun that killed her. She'd been depressed, of course. Her husband had stolen a phone and journals that might be used against her in a custody battle. She stood to lose everything. Who wouldn't start wondering if it was all worth it? Crippled by the emotional pain of a split, who wouldn't think that they might be better off dead? Among the onlookers and emergency personnel the word 'suicide' spread like a forest fire.

For Jenn's family the idea that this vibrant, loving woman who'd made her two sons the centre of her whole universe would take her own life was absurd. Jenn truly believed every day with Dillon and Dalton was a gift and a blessing, so why on earth would she rob herself of the thousands more days which lay ahead of her, the thousands more gifts? It was, quite simply, unthinkable. They knew she had been killed and they knew exactly who had killed her – they just had to prove it.

When Max Barber got to Bogan Gates Drive on that black Saturday morning he was told that Bart Corbin was on his way. Three hours later he still hadn't arrived. 'I was the first family member there at about 5 minutes until 9:00. I waited — I was told by the authorities that Bart was on the way, would be there between 15 and 30 minutes. I waited for three hours. He never showed up. I went back to the authorities two or three times,' recalls Max. 'First I went back to get clothes for my grandchildren and then I went back a second time to find out when they expected Bart to show up at the home. He never came, never made a phone call.'

So here was Barton Corbin – respected community dentist, family man, devoted dad. His wife is dead, apparently suicide, her body found by their oldest child. Did he come rushing back to comfort his heartbroken son? Did he ask where the kids were, who was looking after them, how they were coping? No, he just stayed away. He was silent. And in this silence, the seeds of doubt were allowed to grow. What sort of a father abandons his children at a time like this? The police decided to look more closely into

Dr Barton Corbin's life and past and what they found sent a shock wave through everyone who knew – or rather thought they knew – the 40-year-old dentist.

A few days after Jennifer's death her mother received a phone call. The caller told her that Barton Corbin had been involved with a fellow dental student fourteen years previously who had 'committed suicide' in exactly the same manner. When she died she had also been trying to end her relationship with him. For the Barbers, who'd had no idea of the existence of this former girlfriend, the news was almost too much to take in. It was 'enormous... beyond belief', Narda would later recall.

Dolly Hearn had been a beautiful and vivacious raven-haired young woman when Bart Corbin first met her at dental college in Augusta, Georgia in the late 1980s. He was bowled over by her looks and charm and the way she connected with people – always using their name, always making them feel important. He wasted no time in asking her out. Dolly fitted perfectly into Bart's ambitious master plan – she was attractive, well connected. With her by his side, he'd be well on his way to carving out a glittering career for himself.

A couple of times Dolly took her new boyfriend back to her parent's impressive colonial home in Washington, Georgia. At first Barbara and Carlton Hearn were taken by Bart's quick wit and intelligence but when he told Carlton – also a dentist – that he couldn't wait to graduate so he could 'stick it to people', the Hearns rapidly realised there was a very sinister side to this bright young man. When Dolly confided a few months into the relationship that she and Bart were having troubles and that she was planning to break up with him, her parents couldn't help feeling relieved.

But like everyone else in Bart Corbin's life, the Hearns hadn't recognised the extent of his narcissism and instead attributed it to the typical arrogance of youth. Even the classmates at dental school who'd witnessed his petulant displays of anger when things didn't go his way and his 'explosive temper' didn't fully recognise the deep-rooted self obsession that lay behind his outbursts. They could have no idea then of how a narcissist reacts to rejection, of the rage stirred up when plans are thwarted or the mentality that views lovers as possessions and dictates 'if I can't have her, no one can'.

Soon after trying to end her relationship with Bart, strange, disturbing things started happening to Dolly Hearn. A set of denture casts disappeared from her cubicle at the dental school. Someone put hairspray into her contact lens solution, burning her eyes. A strange pink substance was poured into her gas tank and her tyres deflated. One day someone broke into her apartment and took Tabitha, her cat.

Dolly had no doubt who was responsible. She changed the locks and filed reports with the Richmond County Sheriff's Office, telling officers her ex-boyfriend Bart was behind the campaign. Two weeks after Tabitha disappeared, she told police he'd confessed to having taken the cat and then made a big show of helping to find it. Dolly also went to the Medical College of Georgia with her complaints. The school investigated but concluded no evidence of wrongdoing. Dolly became scared and asked to sleep over at friends' houses rather than stay in her apartment alone. Her anxious father drove to Augusta to tell a recalcitrant Bart to stop harassing his daughter. He also bought her a gun and her brother Carlton took her to the firing range to teach her how to use it.

But then, just as suddenly as it had started, the harassment seemed to stop. Perhaps Bart had finally got the message – or at least Dolly dared hope. Maybe he'd moved on with his life and put the past behind him. For the first time in weeks she stopped looking behind her every five minutes as she walked along the high street or checking the back seat of the car before driving off.

Dolly was back on form. Her smile –which her younger brother Gil described as being able to 'light up a room' and her fellow students just called her 'Dolly Smile' – was firmly back in place. Partway through his speech at his high school graduation, Gil glanced over at his sister to see her beaming in his direction. It's a memory he treasures to this day. Free from the constrictions of Barton Corbin's controlling nature, life was once again full of dazzling potential for Dolly Hearn.

Who knows what the bright, intelligent and attractive Dorothy 'Dolly' Hearn might have made of her life? An able student, she could easily have become the kind of dentist everyone dreams of having – the sort who provides reassurance, support, warmth and who doesn't make you feel stupid for being nervous. She could have been a great mother – Dolly always loved children. She'd have been a fantastic auntie and a devoted daughter to her ageing parents. When a young person dies, all their future selves die with them. That's what makes it so cruel, all that loss of promise.

On the evening of 6 June 1990, Dolly's roommate – Angela Garnto – walked into the living room of their apartment in Augusta to find the 27-year-old sitting up on the sofa with her legs crossed and the gun her father had given her lying in her lap. She had been shot once in the head. Beautiful, vivacious Dolly Hearn had apparently committed suicide.

No one who knew her believed it. She'd taken food out of the freezer to defrost, she'd planned a trip to the beach with family for a few days' time. Then she'd taken a gun and shot herself in the head. Who would buy such a story?

Gil Hearn heard the preposterous news when he got back from a trip with his high school graduating class and found his parents waiting at the airport. 'My Mom said, "We lost our Dolly." It really was the worst thing she could have told me.' The Hearn family had no doubt who was responsible for Dolly's death. 'I knew that Bart had killed her,' Gil Hearn explained later. 'There was never any doubt in my mind, there was never any doubt in my parents' mind.' Plus, there was the witness who'd seen Bart in Dolly's apartment through a crack in the door on the day she died.

But the authorities at the time couldn't come up with any explanation apart from suicide. Subsequent investigations dug up enough doubt to have the suicide verdict thrown into question but still there were insufficient grounds for turning the case into a murder inquiry. The cause of Dolly's death was, in official-speak, inconclusive. Grief-stricken and desperate, the family hired an independent pathologist only to have their hearts ripped apart all over again when no firm evidence of homicide was uncovered and suicide could not be ruled out.

Imagine raising a daughter whose spirit sings, whose laughter touches everybody she meets, who sees every day as a new adventure just waiting to be grasped. Imagine being told this daughter has killed herself even while you know with every breath in your body, that she'd never, ever have contemplated such a thing. Imagine the need you'd have to show the world that your daughter didn't choose to die, that some dark force had snuffed out her life completely against her will. Imagine how that knowledge and those feelings would eat away at you over the years while the world keeps on turning around you and your daughter's friends graduate, get married, have children of their own. Imagine how you'd despair of justice ever being done and dread the thought of going to your grave without the world knowing what really happened to your little girl. That's what Dolly Hearn's parents lived with every day for 14 long years.

They'd all but given up on ever being able to publicly reveal to the world what privately they'd known all along – that Dolly had been murdered – when all of a sudden the news broke about Jennifer Corbin's death in Buford, Georgia just 150 miles away. As the story unfolded live on television, the Hearns could hardly believe what they were seeing. Another woman who'd been trying to end a relationship with Barton Corbin had been found dead from a single gun shot to the head. Another family was starting out on the same nightmare road they'd been travelling for the last 14 years. They were torn between feeling devastated for Jennifer Corbin's family and excited at what the news could mean to their own. For Max and Narda Barber, who'd never known about Dolly or her relationship with Bart, the existence of the Hearns came as a huge shock. It was, said Narda, 'beyond belief.'

There are some moments in time that seem ever so slightly to nudge the world off-kilter so that nothing appears quite the same as it did before and, seen from a new angle, what's passed acquires a whole different meaning. For the Barber family this was one such moment. The son-in-law they'd taken into their lives as one of their own had a mysterious history, one that included a dead girlfriend and a trail of harassment and deception. The man they thought they knew – the father, the husband and the wisecracking friend – turned out to be an illusion. In his place now was a stranger who dressed in the same clothes and drove the same car but looked out at the world from eyes holding completely different secrets. Who knew what he was capable of?

Police investigating Jennifer Corbin's death had begun to question the suicide theory and had started to look on it as a possible homicide. On the night of Jennifer's death Barton had been out with his brother and friends and went back to stay at his brother's afterwards. But there was a brief window of time when he was unaccounted for and they wanted to ask him about it. So far he had not complied with requests to come and be interviewed. All communication was done through his attorney, who remained adamant his client was a grieving widower whose wife, devastated by her failing marriage and forthcoming divorce, had taken her own life.

On the Wednesday following Jennifer's death, her family walked into Flanigan Funeral Home on South Lee Street in Buford to make the necessary arrangements. They'd decided to hold a memorial service followed by a cremation that Friday. At this stage no one in the family had spoken to Barton Corbin, who was staying with his family, so there was disbelief when the funeral director apologetically informed them that Bart, as Jennifer's husband, had arranged for the cremation to take place later that day. In the end all the family could do was ask to see the body and say their goodbyes.

No parent who has brought a child into the world should ever have to sit in the unnatural hush of a funeral home and cradle the lifeless body of that same child, knowing that in the end all the love in the world wasn't enough. No parent should have to whisper goodbye to their child who was supposed to outlive them. When the Barbers left the funeral home that day they were more determined than ever to make sure justice was done for their Jennifer. Of primary concern to the family was the welfare of Dalton and Dillon. The thought of those two boys being returned to the father who'd failed to turn up for them, despite knowing what they'd been through, was more than anyone could bear. The boys had endured the most traumatic of ordeals and were in fear of their father. According to Heather's husband Doug, the first time Corbin had phoned to speak to his oldest son, Dalton started sobbing and refused to stay on the phone. Now, more than ever before, they needed to be surrounded by love. The following day Heather and Doug applied for temporary custody of Dalton and Dillon. To their immeasurable relief, custody was granted.

10 December 2004 – the day of the memorial service –

was dark and stormy. Nevertheless Sugar Hill United Methodist Church in Buford was packed with mourners determined to pay their respects to the woman who'd touched so many lives. No one could believe it when a dark-suited figure with deep-set brown eyes and gaunt cheeks strode into the church and took a seat in the front pew. It was Barton Corbin who, just hours before, had been named as a suspect in Jennifer's death.

What was going through Bart's mind as he sat in that crowded church? Was he asking forgiveness for what he'd done? Was he looking around and finally realising just how many people had loved his wife and how many lives would be devastated by her loss? Or was he too busy worrying about his own future? About whether the police would be able to find any evidence linking him to Jennifer's death, whether he was about to get away with it… again?

Seeing Barton sitting there inscrutably – and, worst of all free – in the front row compounded Jennifer's family's grief still further. When Heather got up in front of the mourners to talk about her sister, she could hardly control her emotions. 'Right now I am so angry,' she said with her voice raw with grief. 'But one thing I know is that love is a million times stronger than anger.'

After the service a well-dressed couple made their way into the room where the Barber family were receiving guests. They were strangers to the rest of the mourners from the tightly knit community and they looked slightly nervous as they introduced themselves to Max and Narda. It was Barbara and Carlton Hearn.

If you've never lost someone you'll never know what grief is, and if you've never lost a child, you'll never understand that most savage strain of grief. The Hearns and the Barbers had this tragic bond in common and more. Each had lost a daughter in the full prime of her life and each believed the same man to be responsible: Barton Corbin.

'There hasn't been a day in the last 14 years where Carlton hasn't talked about Dolly,' Barbara Hearn told Max Barber, taking his hand in hers. Funny that so sad a statement could bring comfort but facing a lifetime without his Jenny and knowing that she would never be far from his thoughts, Max Barber found strength in the knowledge that someone else knew exactly what he was going through.

Exiting the church at the end of this most emotional of afternoons, the mourners were stunned to find the wind and rain of earlier had given way to a perfect rainbow that arched magnificently across the sky. It was, they all agreed, typical of Jenn not to want to leave without sending a message to let them know she was OK. That was just the type of person she was, thoughtful to the last.

After the service the Barbers took Jennifer's ashes back to Heather's house in the candle-shaped urn they'd carefully picked out. The urn was placed on the dining room table surrounded by roses, gerbera daisies and tulips,

Jenn's favourite flower. Her family stood around the table, joined hands and prayed for the woman they'd loved so much. Reaching out a small hand, young Dalton touched the urn that held the ashes of his former life and told his mother how much he missed her. Nothing would ever be the same again.

And yet still the word 'suicide' hung heavy in the air over Gwinnett County. Police may have decided to treat this as a homicide investigation, but Barton Corbin's supporters were having none of it. It was very sad, they said, but here was a woman teetering on the brink of divorce, distraught at the thought of all she had to lose. People had killed themselves for less. Barton himself stayed out of the way, indirectly proclaiming his innocence, while refusing to come in voluntarily for questioning.

Without further evidence it seemed like a stalemate — except for one thing. Vibrant, positive-thinking women like Dolly and Jenn don't tend to commit suicide — and certainly not by shooting themselves in the head and not without leaving some sort of note. You didn't have to be Einstein to work out that the odds against a man being involved with two women who kill themselves in exactly that manner were pretty high.

The police decided to keep a close watch on Barton. They still hadn't been able to trace the gun back to Corbin's friend Richard Wilson, but it wasn't long before investigators decided the blood trail and the angle of the bullet wound at the scene of Jennifer's death weren't consistent with suicide. Plus Jenn didn't have any gun powder residue on her fingers. Add that to Barton's strange behaviour regarding the children after Jenn's death and the good dentist was starting to look ever so slightly suspicious.

Meanwhile, back in Augusta Dolly's case was reopened following the developments in Gwinnett County. Using newer technology, the authorities again looked at photographs taken at the scene and in particular at the blood spatter patterns. This time the conclusion was very different: the body had been manipulated *after* the wound had been inflicted. The net was closing in on Corbin. The prosecution put a tap on Bart's phone. In one conversation he referred to Dolly as that 'bitch in Augusta'. Who hasn't said things in an unguarded moment that they might later regret? But to describe a dead former girlfriend in such a derogatory way pointed to a sinister side to Bart that most people had never suspected he was capable of.

On Wednesday 22 December – Barton Corbin's 41st birthday – he was arrested for his part in the death of Dolly Hearn. Three police vehicles surrounded the white Chevrolet Suburban in which the dentist was travelling near his office on Braselton Highway. With him was his secretary. It was a very sudden and very public arrest, which was shown live on TV – the ultimate humiliation for such a control freak. Two weeks later he was charged with murdering his wife.

For the best part of the following two years, Barton maintained he was innocent, the unfortunate victim of a freak coincidence. His family – twin brother Brad, younger brother Robert and mother Constance – stood by him. Bart hired the best defence lawyers available, charging them with proving he was actually a grieving husband being made to suffer horribly for becoming romantically involved with two emotionally unstable women. In the end, said defence lawyer David Wolfe, relationship breakdown was the villain in this tragedy, not Dr Barton Corbin:'You ask anybody what does a divorce do to people emotionally? It's heart-wrenching, it's gut-wrenching, it's one of the things that drives people to take their lives or attempt to take their lives.'

For the Hearns and the Barbers it was nearly two years of limbo in which their everyday lives coexisted as though in parallel universe with their new lives as families of the victims. Some days it was almost possible to lose yourself in the routine of school runs, baseball practice, grocery shopping and work, and to believe that life was once again back to normal. Other days even getting up out of bed seemed too monumental a task. Always, over-hanging everything – every birthday celebration, every holiday and every family meal – was the shadow of Barton Corbin and the possibility that he just might get away with it again.

The trial was scheduled for the second week in September 2006. On 12 September, the second day of jury selection, came the breakthrough. The lead prosecutor was handed a note by his chief investigator: 'Come out of the courtroom now'. The words were underlined for extra emphasis. 'This had better be good,' he thought to himself as he made his excuses to leave the room. And it was. The gun that shot Jennifer Corbin had finally been traced back to Troy, Alabama, and Richard Wilson had confessed to giving it to Corbin. It was the piece of evidence that smashed a hole through Barton's carefully constructed dam of lies.

Bart now knew there was no hope of getting off, but still there was a chance for damage limitation. His legal team was told that if he confessed to the murders of both women, he'd be spared the death penalty. For an egocentric such as Corbin, who truly believed the world existed only so far as he himself there was really no choice.

On Friday, 15 September Barton Corbin faced a judge and the two families whose lives he'd destroyed and listened impassively as the details of the murders were outlined by the District Attorney. Then it was his turn to speak, which he did in a voice devoid of emotion.

'I'm Barton Thomas Corbin. 12.22.63 is my date of birth. I'm 42 years old.'

'Do you fully understand all of the charges against you in the case?' He was asked. 'Yes,' he replied.

'Has anyone used force or threats against you to plead guilty against your will?'

'No,' was his curt response.

Then came the exchange everyone had come to hear: 'Did you in fact commit the offence of malice murder to which you are now pleading guilty as it is outlined in the indictment?'

This was the moment the families had been waiting for – the Barbers for 2 years, the Hearns for 16 – but would he actually go through with it? Would this arch manipulator and most calculating game player finally put an end to their torment or would he change his mind and drag it out, even if it meant risking his own life in the pursuit of ruining theirs? Their answer came in just one short glorious word.

'Yes.'

It was over. The sentence was to be two life terms served concurrently.

Asked in the courtroom whether he had anything to say, Corbin declined but his victims' families took the chance to address the court and the world's media that had become engrossed in this case. 'Bart Corbin has disgraced his profession and has stolen from mankind,' said Dolly's brother Carlton Jnr. '16 years of silence, 16 years of pain.'

Jennifer Corbin's father Max Barber clearly struggled with conflicting emotions as he faced the man who had robbed him of his daughter yet would be forever linked to the family as the father of his two small grandsons and the son-in-law he'd once loved. 'The broken hearts of the Barber family, the Hearn family and the Corbin family can't be measured,' he told Bart. 'The hearts are going to mend. I can't speak about your heart... what's going to happen to you. God might forgive you – I never will. I speak for my family when I say I just virtually hope you burn in hell.'

★ ★ ★ ★ ★

On Bogan Gates Drive nestling between two houses there now stands a small park where children play and their mothers sometimes picnic on hot summer days. The granite marker in one corner of the park reads 'Dedicated in loving memory of our friend and neighbour Jennifer Barber Corbin'.

Are the dead really gone when so much of them remains in all they leave behind – in the laughter of their children, in the hearts of their families, in the very grass of the park that now bears their name? Barton Corbin hated the thought of divorce because he loathed the idea of losing anything he considered 'his'. The irony is that in seeking to exercise the ultimate control over his wife, he ended up setting her spirit free while he himself faces the rest of his life locked up in a cell, a prisoner of his own ruthless ego. It is, after all, some kind of justice.

CHAPTER THREE

CROCODILE
TEARS

With his large, tortoise-shell framed glasses, dark suit, crisp white shirt and solemn demeanour, 44-year-old Garry Malone looked every inch the anxious husband as he made an impassioned television appeal for information regarding his missing wife, Sharon. His voice cracked with emotion as he entreated Sharon to get in touch, if not for his sake at least for their two young sons. 'The boys are asking for Mum,' he said, looking directly into the television cameras. 'Please contact the police or your Dad and put our minds at rest.'

It was December 1999 and 28-year-old Sharon — a trainee teacher — had disappeared from the family home in Cranborne Crescent, Potters Bar one month before. No one had heard from her since. No wonder Garry was frantic with worry. His eyes welled with tears as he sat behind the press conference table, flanked by police and Sharon's father, Harry Clinch, and begged for an end to his family's nightmare. With his expensive-looking gold watch and his well-groomed, closely-cut hair, Garry was doing what any respectable, loving husband would do in the same situation – except that it was all a sham.

Even as he leaned across towards the TV microphones and pleaded with Sharon to come home, he was well aware that there was no chance of that ever happening. Because Garry knew exactly where his wife of six years was – lying dead in a dried-up stream bed in a Hertfordshire country park. It's hard to imagine how a husband who once proposed marriage and who held his wife so tenderly after she gave birth to their beautiful babies could put on such a performance all the time knowing the truth about the terrible thing he'd done to her. How could a man who'd faced the same woman at the breakfast table every morning for the past few years, who lay beside her every night hearing her breathing softly, appeal so sincerely for her to get in touch, knowing that no one would ever hear from her again?

Partners who have affairs are often surprised how easy they can compartmentalise their affair from their normal life so the two remain separate and guilt is kept at bay. Perhaps this is how Garry Malone managed to look straight at the TV cameras and send a heart-felt message to his wife without betraying any hint of the horrors that must still have lurked in his memory. Or perhaps, as the papers at the time decided, he really was devoid of a conscience and when his gaze met that of the TV audiences, we were all staring straight into a remorseless void in which ruthlessness, rage and greed echoed without hope of redemption.

It was certainly a side of Malone that Sharon wouldn't have believed possible when she first met him as an impressionable teenager. Garry was a karate instructor at Queen Elizabeth Girls' School in Barnet and, like many a young male teacher in the rarefied atmosphere, he suddenly found himself the focus of much giggling speculation. For a solid, average-looking man with the heavy jowl look of someone a lot older, the attention was an ego boost and he enjoyed giving classes and chatting to his young pupils, including 14-year-old Sharon.

At the time Garry was married and for a few years the relationship between awkward teenager and her older instructor remained a platonic friendship. They chatted about martial arts, about things that were going on in the school. But that all changed after Garry's divorce. What had started out as an oddly paired friendship deepened into romance and finally, in 1993, to marriage. A 16-year age gap can cause problems in a marriage, however. Where one partner has so much more life experience than the other, then the balance of power between the two can get permanently skewed. Where one partner grows up within the confines of the relationship, the potential for growing apart increases. There's a danger of one being forced into the role of parent and the other being the errant child. It's not a healthy basis for an equal, loving relationship.

Did that happen with Garry and Sharon? No one can be sure but the relationship was tricky almost from the start. Garry Malone had never really been what you'd call career-minded. After teaching karate he'd gone on to buying and selling rare guitars and had built up a valuable collection. Then he'd got a job for under £12,000 a year selling water coolers. Often he was overdrawn at the bank and owed money on credit cards. Yet he showed no real motivation to get a better-paid job to try and pay off some of his debts. 'There's nothing that's really "right" for me,' he'd complain.

Even though she'd always been far more ambitious than her husband, Sharon had chosen to give up her job as a fire research scientist to train as a teacher so that she'd have the school holidays free for her children. She was OK with that decision but it meant that she too wasn't able to contribute much to the family coffers. 'Wouldn't it be great to have a partner who supported you so it didn't matter if you were working or not?' she'd fantasise to friends.

Lack of financial security invariably creates problems in a marriage. Is one partner spending too much? And is the other holding on too tightly to the purse strings? Should one have made more provisions for saving, should the other not have insisted on buying the house or the car, or the gym membership? Relationship experts cite money as one of the greatest sources of conflict among couples. Garry and Sharon certainly had their share of arguments about it.

There were other factors too in the Malones' marriage that point to a relationship in trouble. Garry had problems completely trusting his much younger wife. Sometimes when she went out he'd drive himself crazy thinking about where she was, often quizzing her best friend Paula Fiddes about what she'd been up to. 'I don't know why you get so wound up about it,' Sharon would tell him. 'I'm not doing anything wrong.' But her protestations did little to reassure Garry's naturally suspicious mind.

Though both Garry and Sharon adored their two sons – Adam, born three years into the marriage, and Robert, who came along two years later – the boys' births couldn't stop the cracks in the relationship from deepening. Sometimes children can bring a splintering couple closer together. Other times their births are like a sticking plaster applied to a severely wounded relationship. It might just hold it for a time but if it's bad enough then sooner or later the wound will just open up again.

By summer 1999 Garry and Sharon Malone both knew their relationship was in big trouble yet neither of them wanted to upset the children or deal with the financial nightmare that dismantling a family entails. 'We can't keep going on like this though,' they both acknowledged. They decided on a trial separation. For Sharon this was a chance to look more closely at the marriage and find out what had been going wrong. But for Garry it was an opportunity to consider something (or someone) else entirely: Paula Fiddes, Sharon's supposed best friend.

Garry used time off from his marriage to immerse himself in an affair with Sharon's old school pal. One thing he was very clear about, though: his wife must never, ever find out. The open-ended separation provided the perfect smoke screen in which the affair could flourish undetected. It was great to be able to admit to Paula how unhappy he was in his marriage. 'I've told Sharon we'd both be better off if one of us was dead,' he confessed. Before too long, however, the Malones had changed their minds about separation and decided to reconcile. This was around the time that Sharon's mother died. Garry had been a big support during her mother's illness, even giving shiatsu massage to the ailing woman. So naturally, Sharon turned to her estranged husband following her bereavement. Garry went back to the marital home and the relationship with Fiddes was effectively over.

Yet infidelity plays subtle tricks on a marriage. The things you once thought were solid and measurable turn out to be illusions, lightly sketched holograms of real beliefs and emotions. Back home in Cranborne Crescent, Potters Bar, Garry Malone couldn't quite settle. After more than a decade with Sharon, he'd rediscovered what it was like to feel desire again, and to be desired. He'd had a taste of freedom and he liked it. But Garry was nothing if not realistic. He knew that divorce from Sharon would mean the end of life as he knew it. The house wasn't exactly a palace but it was a nice area where kids played outside. The fact that Potters Bar Golf Course was just over the railway line at the back and the George V playing fields were a short hop away in front gave it a countrified feel, too. Divorce would put an end to all that.

Garry was in a difficult position. He knew he wanted out of his marriage but he hated the thought of being plunged into poverty and maybe forced to get an apartment somewhere, seeing the boys only once in a while. If only Sharon would be reasonable, he thought. If she'd just agree things weren't right between them and accept perhaps around £45,000 as a divorce payment – half the value of their home – they could work out a way through this mess and forge a new kind of relationship. Sharon, however, had other ideas.

She'd also been thinking about divorce and talking to friends. According to her calculations, a figure of £100,000 was far more appropriate to her situation. And if Garry claimed not to have that sort of money, why he could just sell off a few of his precious guitars. He was always droning on about how valuable they were. Well, here was a chance to prove it. Except that Garry had already made it impossible to cash in on his guitar collection. The year before he'd put in an insurance claim, saying thieves had stolen the collection and claiming a massive £360,000 in compensation. In reality he knew where the guitars were stashed but it wasn't as though he could auction them off – not unless he wanted to be done for insurance fraud.

Garry Malone felt as if he was caught between a rock and a hard place. He'd had a taste of bachelor life during his separation and he'd loved it. His marriage, meanwhile, was becoming increasingly uncomfortable. The air in the Cranborne Crescent house was dense with resentment and untold secrets. Garry had never confessed to Sharon about his relationship with Paula Fiddes but still the affair inhabited the house like an uninvited lodger, getting in the way of any attempts at reconciliation and leaving a sour atmosphere in its wake. After an affair is discovered, the betrayed partner will often feel almost a sense of relief. 'I knew something was up,' they'll say. 'There was just something different about them, something alien.' The adulterer may feel that they're behaving perfectly normally, but still something will rankle and jar, creating permanent tension in the relationship.

Garry knew his marriage couldn't survive much longer but he also knew he'd be facing financial disaster if Sharon pushed through a divorce claim. Even worse, he risked losing custody of the boys who had always lit up his life even in the darkest days of his marriage – and things would only get worse if his affair with Paula Fiddes ever became public knowledge.

The relationship curdled in the air around the warring couple. On 27 November, Sharon met up with a friend and confessed she wished she'd never agreed to try again. 'Going back to Garry is the biggest mistake I've made,' she confided, obviously angry with herself for having weakened.

Imagine what an emotional pressure cooker the Cranborne Crescent house must have become. Imagine how the bitterness – suppressed for the sake of the boys – must have built up. Who knows what it was in the end that finally sparked the fire that had been building up in that dried-up tinderbox of a relationship all those months and years. Did Sharon find out about Garry's affair? Did she tell him she'd finally had enough and was going to file for a divorce settlement that gave her and the kids the kind of financial recompense she felt she deserved? No one except Garry Malone will ever know what took place in the bedroom of that Potters Bar house one Sunday night. All that's certain is that Sharon Malone, fitness fanatic and devoted mother of two, disappeared from the world's radar on 28 November 1999. The next time anyone would see her, she would already have been dead for months – bludgeoned around the head with a blunt object and left to rot in a dried-out stream.

Over the days following Sharon's disappearance, Garry gave a bravura performance as the concerned husband. In the first act of this carefully choreographed drama, he played a man whose wife has walked out on him. Everyone knew they'd been rowing and no one would be surprised if Sharon wanted a bit of time on her own away from her disintegrating marriage. After waiting a day or two, he rang Sharon's teacher training college. 'I just wanted to know if Sharon has turned up?' he asked, just as a slightly anxious husband who's had a row with his wife might do. 'I haven't seen her for a couple of days and I'm starting to get worried.' Of course, the answer was no. With mock humility, he told police that he thought Sharon had left him. Things hadn't been too good at home, he explained. They probably saw this type of thing all the time.

But as the days went on with no contact from the missing woman, Garry shifted his performance up a notch. Now he was no longer the deserted but resigned husband but instead he played the actively worried citizen. He hinted heavily that Sharon had owed money to some 'nasty people', which is why she'd disappeared. To reinforce his argument, he persuaded Paula Fiddes to tell police that she'd met up with Sharon on the night she disappeared and handed over a bag she'd held for safekeeping, which contained money, a passport and 'something squidgy'.

Paula later claimed she hadn't liked lying, but she thought that Garry was, in her words, a 'nice, gentle bloke' and she wanted to help him out if she could. The fabricated story didn't wash with anyone who'd known bright, sporty Sharon Malone, but it bought Garry Malone more, much-needed time.

In December 1999 Garry gave the performance of his

life at an emotional press conference where he pleaded for his missing wife to come home. The hearts of TV viewers everywhere went out to him as he struggled to keep his emotions under control in front of the cameras. No wonder he had struggled to hold down a career – he'd obviously missed his true vocation: acting. That same month a police search of the Cranborne Crescent house unearthed letters, purportedly from a private investigator, providing evidence that Sharon was responsible for the disintegration of the marriage. The letters later turned out to be written by Garry himself.

In the weeks following Sharon's disappearance, the true picture of the perilous state of the couple's relationship began to emerge and police suspicions became increasingly focused on Garry himself. But he knew the net was closing on him and that if Sharon's body was discovered no amount of acting was going to get him off the hook. All around him the world was celebrating the new Millennium. It was a time for fresh starts so Garry Malone decided to have one of his own.

On 21 January 2000 he withdrew £30,000 from various bank accounts and loaded some of his prize belongings into a rented Mercedes van. Then, with his two small sons strapped in the back, he set off for Spain to begin a new life. The Costa del Sol has become a magnet for British citizens looking to escape from pressures at home. With its long stretches of beaches and highly developed resorts, all boasting a massive expat population and all the comforts of home, it's the perfect place to reinvent yourself.

Britons flee to the Costa del Sol for many reasons: as a last attempt to save a flagging marriage or perhaps a way out of a marriage that's already dead; to escape debt or high-stress jobs and even because they're wanted by the police. Not for nothing has the Costa del Sol become known as the Costa del Crime. In 1978, a century-old extradition treaty between Spain and the UK expired and created a loophole whereby crooks could hide out on the Costas without fear of being hauled back home. In 1985, the treaty was replaced, perhaps with a view to Spain joining the EU the following year, so the loophole was closed up. But the image of the Costa Del Sol as a sanctuary for Briton's criminal classes – a place where they could disappear into anonymity and become just another new British face amid hundreds of thousands more all looking to start a new life in the sun – remained.

Some people arrive totally cold and have to build up a whole social network from scratch. But Garry Malone was lucky. When he arrived on the Costa with his two young sons in late January 2000, he already had a friend to show him the ropes. Her name was Roberta Kirque. Within weeks, he had found somewhere to live in the heavily built-up stretch of coast between Malaga and Fuengirola and enrolled the children in local schools. And he had a new identity to go with his new life: he was now Ralph Kirque.

Still he couldn't bring himself to leave his old life entirely behind. He sent letters from Spain to Paula Fiddes and to Sharon's heart-broken father Harry, who'd lost his wife to cancer, his daughter had disappeared and now he'd had his two precious grandsons taken away from him as well. The letters were full of justification for leaving: Garry was still sticking to his story about Sharon owing money to the wrong sort of people. 'I'm scared what would happen if I came back,' he said.

If you're forced to flee your home, southern Spain isn't a bad place to live out your exile. Garry quickly came to appreciate the 300-plus days a year of sunshine and the open disregard for the law endemic in this part of the world. There were weekends on the beach and long evenings sitting outside sea-front bars watching the sun set through the fronds of the palm trees. And finally, he had someone with whom he truly connected to share these experiences – his new girlfriend Marie Idden. Life was pretty good.

Back in the UK, though, things were looking anything but sunny for Garry Malone. On 18 March 2000, after two frustrating months when it seemed as if the investigation into Sharon Malone's disappearance had all but ground to a halt, a member of the public stumbled across a most unpleasant discovery in North Mymms Park, Hertfordshire. Lying in the bed of a dried-up stream amongst dense woodland was the partially clothed, decomposing body of a woman: it was Sharon. Finally the case turned from missing person to murder inquiry with just one prime suspect.

When the news about Sharon's death was out, Garry Malone declared he'd cried bucket loads and maybe he did. But were his tears for his dead wife, or for himself? The discovery of the body opened up whole new evidence to investigating police officers. Garry knew that sooner or later the evidence would lead straight back to him. His carefully spun web of deceit started to unravel when Paula Fiddes was arrested. Her story of seeing Sharon Malone the night she died had now been exposed as a tissue of lies and police had some serious questions for her. Fiddes later claimed in court to have been 'scared' by the news of her former friend's death because she'd realised what her ex-lover was capable of. This time she told the police that she'd actually met Garry Malone on the night of Sharon's murder. He'd called her to say he'd fallen off his bike and needed bandages and water. She also said Garry had gone on to give her 'lists of things to say'.

More lies came to light when mobile phone records revealed Garry Malone to have been in the area of North Mymms Park on the night of the murder. Detectives appealed to him to come forward and 'help clear things up'. But Garry Malone – aka Ralph Kirque – had no intention of giving up his easy life in the sun for what would almost certainly be immediate arrest and incarceration. Through his older son Gareth, the child of his first marriage, he told the media that he wasn't prepared to come back and see his two small sons taken into care while he faced a prison sentence for a crime he insisted he hadn't committed.

'I don't think he will be coming back,' Gareth told reporters on the second anniversary of Sharon's death. 'The police have not been helpful to him – if they had, I'm sure he would have returned.'

As Ralph Kirque, Garry had things pretty good. Although at first his kids had found it hard, gradually they'd settled and learned to speak fluent Spanish as small children tend to do when thrown in at the deep end of a different culture. They'd even briefly re-discovered their doting grandfather, Harry Clinch, who'd flown out for a tearful reunion just before Christmas 2001 – although Garry had made sure there wasn't any contact after that. The last thing he wanted was a constant link to Sharon and the murder inquiry intruding on his brave new world.

But deep inside Garry knew he was living on borrowed time. He might have been enjoying a dream life, but the nightmare of the past was never far from the surface. Even the sunniest days bear a shadow if you're constantly looking behind you to see who's coming. The most beautiful of surroundings can look sinister if you're always wondering why that car is moving so slowly or that group of men are looking in your direction. Was there a sense then in which the end might finally have come as some sort of relief for a man who'd worn his secret for so long? Who knows?

On 31 May 2003 the knock on the door that he had been expecting for years finally came. Garry was arrested and taken to Madrid to appear before magistrates. He was then detained in a high security unit in the Spanish capital while the extradition wrangles began.

Though the extradition laws between Spain and the UK are now back in place following the brief lapse of the late 1970s and early 1980s, the process is complex and time consuming. Anyone with a good lawyer can drag the whole thing out for months. Knowing that he could face the rest of his life in prison if his case went before a British court, Garry Malone wasn't in any rush to get home. He managed to stretch out the extradition process for the maximum 15 months. In the meantime he married his girlfriend Marie Idden.

It's hard to see how this by now 50-year-old man with thinning hair and a paunch, who was already behind bars and facing a lifetime in prison for the alleged murder of his wife might have struck anyone as good husband material. But love does funny things to people.

By the beginning of June 2004 Garry's legal representatives had finally run out of time – and luck. He was back in the UK on 6 June and in Hendon Magistrates Court where he pleaded not guilty to murdering his wife. Beside him was his son Gareth Malone who'd been accused of disposing of bloodstained wallpaper from the Cranborne Crescent house. Also present was Paula Fiddes.

By this stage Paula had little to say to her former lover. The man she'd claimed to find 'nice' and 'gentle' was proving to be anything but. In fact it occurred to her that she herself had had a very lucky escape.

Nearly a year passed between Garry's arrival back in the UK and the start of his murder trial. How galling it must have been to be locked up inside a light-starved prison cell, to look back on those languid days in Spain, soaking up the Andalucian sun and to realise that life might now be closed to you for good. How dreary must the English skies have appeared through the prison bars – layer upon layer of grey, each one more soul-destroying than the last.

Finally, on 16 March 2005 Garry Malone stood trial for the murder of his wife Sharon five and a half years before. In court was Harry Clinch, still grieving for his dead daughter and the grandsons he yearned to see. Harry knew the peace of mind he'd enjoyed before 1999 would never return, but at least he might get some answers. That was the most he could hope for.

The court case at London's Old Bailey dragged on for almost two months. Finally, after 22 hours of deliberation, Garry Malone was found guilty of murder by a majority verdict. Unlike his performance in front of the TV cameras all those years before, Garry showed no emotion as the verdict was read out. He stared impassively ahead of him as if the jury foreman's voice was just background noise.

Over the next few days Garry's son Gareth was found

not guilty of disposing of evidence from the Potters Bar house. In Paula Fiddes' case, the jury failed to reach a verdict on the allegation that she helped Malone, but she was later given a fine and an 8-month suspended sentence for perverting the course of justice by lying to police.

A week after the original verdict was reached, Malone was back in court to receive a life sentence. 'You are a manipulative, calculating and deceitful man,' Judge Stephen Kramer told him. For Harry Clinch and the rest of Sharon's family it was the outcome they'd been hoping for although it did little to fill the jagged hole left in their lives by Sharon's death. 'I have got to get some answers,' Harry pleaded outside the courthouse. 'I want to know why he did it.'

But the legacy of Garry Malone's crime extends far beyond his victim's family. Anyone who saw that original TV appeal, who watched a cold-blooded killer play the part of a desperate husband with such consummate ease will have been left with a bitter aftertaste. If the very person who swore to love and honour could go on to commit murder and then lie about it so well and with so little conscience, what's the point in getting close to someone? Do you ever really know what the person who shares your life and your bed is capable of?

And that's the worst thing about crimes such as Garry Malone's: they force us to ask that most destructive and hurtful of all questions – can we ever really trust anybody?

CHAPTER FOUR

PAID FOR HIS OWN DEATH

Yvette Luffman nervously counted through the stack of money in front of her. She'd already been through it at least twice before but she wanted to make sure it was all there. Plus, she needed to have something to do to take her mind off the enormity of what she was doing. To be honest, there was a big part of her that still didn't believe she would really go through with it. It was as if she was watching a film – only the lead actress was herself. Things like this just didn't happen in real life did they? Still, if it was a film then she could just switch it off at any time and walk away, couldn't she? And everything would go back to how it was.

Once again her shaky fingers sorted out the sheaf of notes into piles. Yes, it was all there. She got out an envelope and stuffed the money inside. It was amazing how thick the bundle seemed. The envelope was so full, the flap would barely close over the top.

One thousand pounds. It was such a lot of money. Just think of all the things she could do with that amount of cash. She could get the kids the bits and pieces they were constantly asking for and buy some new clothes; she could even put some money down on a holiday somewhere exotic. She wouldn't care where it was as long as it was well away from the Midlands.

Not that Boston − where she'd lived up until then − wasn't a decent place to live. With its historic buildings, vast parish church and busy market, the attractive town was a great place to bring up children. Now she'd met new boyfriend Wayne, however, she'd been spending much more time in his hometown of Bulwell, Nottinghamshire, which wasn't at all as picturesque. Besides, since her marriage break up and all the rows that had followed it, every place seemed to carry some bitter memory. A thousand quid would get her well away from here.

Still, it was no good thinking like that, she told herself sternly, sealing up the envelope and smoothing it down decisively. She knew she couldn't spend a penny of that money; she just had to bide her time and wait. Before long she'd have loads of money and then she could do all the things she dreamed of − have the holiday of a lifetime if she wanted to. She remembered when she'd got the money from Simon, her ex-husband. It was supposed to be the first down payment on the £4,000 he owed her as part of their divorce settlement. Funny how the other £3,000 had never materialised though she lost track of the number of times she'd asked him about it. He'd been going out practically every night so it wasn't as if he couldn't afford it. Well, she wasn't married to him any more and he'd messed her about for the very last time. As she slipped the bulging envelope into her handbag, Yvette wondered what Simon would say had he known just how she planned to spend the money he'd given her.

★ ★ ★ ★ ★

Making her way through Nottingham City Centre with her boyfriend Wayne Briscoe, Yvette noticed he looked ill at ease with his unhealthy complexion even more pasty-looking than normal.

'You sure he's going to be there?' she asked him again.

He nodded curtly.

As they approached Chambers Bar at the corner of Maid Marian Way, the karaoke for which it was famous was already in full swing and someone was belting out the words to an old R&B classic. Chambers was one of Yvette and Wayne's regular haunts and normally the couple would have gone in for a drink and to have a good giggle at the singers, but tonight they weren't in any mood for socialising.

'Is that him?' whispered Yvette, indicating the bouncer standing outside the entrance to the bar. Once again Wayne nodded.

The man on the door was Thomas Convery. Wayne, who'd also worked as a bouncer, had come across him through work. He didn't know him that well, but he knew his reputation. If you wanted something doing that wasn't exactly legal, Thomas Convery was your man – as long as you had the cash to make it worth his while. With her heart hammering hard, Yvette edged towards the dour-looking doorman.

'I've heard you're the sort of person who'll do, erm, certain things for money,' she said, agitatedly. Thomas gazed at her coldly. He knew exactly what she was talking about, but he gave nothing away. 'I assume these things you're talking about are illegal?' he asked. Yvette's nerves made her talk faster than normal as she agreed and then went on to explain what she wanted. 'I need someone killed,' she said, the words tumbling out in a rush.

Her request was really quite simple. She wanted Thomas Convery to kill her ex husband. The bouncer listened as Yvette recounted her story. Then he had a question: 'How will I know what he looks like?' Wayne and Yvette looked at one another. This part was easy. 'Come here,' Yvette commanded. She led the way to a window that looked from the street into the bar and then she pointed to a man sitting inside. 'That's him,' she said. 'That's Simon.' Convery stared in at the man he'd been told to kill. He recognised him as a regular in the bar. He'd always been friendly, jovial even. Still, business was business. 'OK,' he assented.

After that there were a few details to thrash out. Thomas Convery's price tag for murder turned out to be £30,000. Yvette arranged that she would put the money she had received for her unofficial divorce settlement as a down payment and would pay the rest when Simon's house was sold following his death. She had worked out that his house was worth over £200,000. Even after the mortgage had been paid off there'd be the best part of £100,000 left. In addition, she and Wayne committed to providing Convery with the murder weapon plus a diagram of the layout of Simon's house and a breakdown of his daily routine.

That was the summer of 2003. The next time Yvette and Wayne met with Thomas Convery – at another bar where he was working – they had with them the envelope stuffed with cash. It was the £1,000 Simon Luffman had gave to his ex-wife. In effect, he was bankrolling his own execution.

Yvette wanted the murder carried out before 23 October. On that day she was due to give evidence against her ex-husband in connection with a minor drugs trial and was anxious to avoid the experience. Though her separation from Simon a couple of years before had been largely amicable and they'd continued to see each other socially because of the son they shared, as well as her other children who'd always got on well with him, since then their relationship had been very volatile. Money was a constant source of tension. Instead of a formal divorce settlement sorted by lawyers, the Luffmans had informally agreed to the £4,000 payment. And when Simon had dragged his feet about paying up, it had caused major rows, with both of them making threats against the other. Yvette didn't at all relish the prospect of standing up in court against her ex-husband.

She and Wayne supplied Thomas Convery with a shotgun and ammunition as well as copies of the keys to the front door of Simon's house and a description of his car. Their idea was that Convery should kill Simon in his home and make it look like a failed robbery.

What passed through Yvette's mind as she painstakingly went through the details of her ex-husband's routine with the man she'd hired to kill him? Did the fact that someone else was carrying out the deed make it seem somehow less real? Did she tell herself that she could pull out at any time and say she'd changed her mind? Or did she just divorce herself from the murder in the same way that she'd divorced herself from the victim himself? It's unlikely that we will ever know. What is known, however, is that Thomas Convery decided he didn't like the idea of killing Simon Luffman in his own home in Langley Mill. Instead, on 19 October he invented a drugs deal in an intricate plan designed to lure Yvette's ex-husband to a disused section of Nottingham Canal, off Coventry Lane in Wollaton.

Now mostly used by walkers and nature lovers as well as the occasional fisherman, this is a scenic spot. If you want an area that's accessible but where the chances of being spotted are slim, you couldn't do much better than here, where the barely used towpath is flanked by a screen of trees providing privacy and blocking off any chance of escape. Simon Luffman would have assumed his shady new acquaintance had picked this spot to make sure they could talk well away from prying eyes. It would never have crossed his mind that the seclusion of the towpath at Wollaton was also perfect for disguising the sound of gunfire.

By the time Thomas Convery walked away from the Nottingham Canal, Simon Luffman was lying dead on the ground. He had been shot four times with a sawn-off shotgun: twice in the head and twice in the back. His body was found the next day. The murder of Simon Luffman caused a stir around the Nottingham bars and clubs where he'd been a well-known face. It wasn't long before attention became focused on Thomas Convery, who was known to have talked to Luffman shortly before he was killed.

'Yeah, I knew him – he was a regular in the bar,' Convery told police. 'Nice bloke, friendly.' Convery's story was that Simon Luffman had approached him about a potential business deal he had coming up. Something about it sounded slightly dodgy and he thought he might need a bodyguard. In the end, Convery insisted, he'd got cold feet and had decided not to go along with it. That's when

Simon Luffman had been killed. But detectives weren't buying Convery's story, particularly not after traces of Luffman's blood were found on his trainers.

In December 2004 Thomas Convery went on trial at Nottingham Crown Court for the murder of Simon Luffman. Though he continued to protest his innocence, he was found guilty of murder and jailed for a minimum of 20 years. In court to see justice done and acting every inch the grieving widow was Yvette Luffman. Sat in the dock, struggling with the knowledge that he'd spend the next two decades of his life in prison, Convery felt a growing sense of rage as he watched Yvette comforting her ex-husband's grief-stricken mother. The hypocrisy of it took his breath away. How could she act so concerned and upset when she was the one who'd masterminded the whole thing?

Over the next few days and weeks Convery's sense of injustice grew. At this point he was in his early thirties. He had a girlfriend, a job and a full life. By the time he was released from prison he'd be middle-aged and all that would be lost to him. Yet Wayne Briscoe and Yvette Luffman got to go about their lives as if nothing had happened. It was so unfair. Locked up in his cell, Thomas Convery had plenty of time to brood on what had happened. The more he thought about it, the stronger became his resolve that Luffman and Briscoe should pay for the murder, just as he was doing. He decided to confess.

The police had long since been convinced that the murder of Simon Luffman was a contract killing. Until that point they just hadn't had the evidence to arrest anyone. Now they set about building a case against his ex-wife and her lover. In January 2007 Yvette Luffman and Wayne Briscoe went on trial for the murder of Simon Luffman. Like Wayne, Yvette protested her innocence throughout the trial, claiming Simon's murder had devastated herself, their son and his whole family. Her repeated denials fell on stony ears, however.

On 7 February 2007 a jury at Birmingham Crown Court found the pair guilty of murder. They were sentenced to life imprisonment and will also have to serve a minimum of 20 years. 'They share as much blame for Mr Luffman's murder as Thomas Convery, who pulled the trigger,' said the Chief Prosecutor. Yvette never admitted any part in the murder, insisting she'd never 'paid a single penny' towards having her ex-husband killed and that she'd been greatly affected by his death.

Is there some part of her mind that actually believes this twisted version of events; that continues, despite the evidence against her, to cling to the image of herself as the wronged widow, the long-suffering mother of a bereaved child? One thing's for sure, as she starts out on her life sentence Yvette Luffman will have a very long time to reconcile herself to the truth.

CHAPTER FIVE

LE LORD
DISPARU

Anthony Ashley-Cooper, 10th Earl of Shaftesbury, smiled shyly at his new bride. Nearly 25 years his junior, with soft brown eyes and a wild mane of brown-blonde hair, to the 63-year-old Earl Jamila M'Barek seemed be a tantalising mass of contradictions. Overtly sexy as her job in a hostess bar demanded, she also loved to play the homemaker, cooking up delicious meals and serving them to him as though his comfort mattered to her more than anything else. A relatively well off divorcee in her own right, she also seemed gratifyingly impressed by his aristocratic background and substantial inherited wealth. Not yet 40, she was young enough to satisfy his taste for youthful, exotic-looking models yet not so young that she made him look like a dirty – and foolish – old man. Overall, the Earl was infatuated with his Tunisian-Dutch wife and convinced that despite already having two failed marriages behind him, this time it really would be third time lucky.

It was November 2002 and they'd returned to the south of France, which they had both come to regard as home, after getting married in Holland. The sun dancing across the surface of the turquoise Mediterranean seemed to reinforce the optimism Anthony felt inside. Here he was – a wealthy man with few responsibilities – living on the French Riviera's glorious Côte d'Azur with its luxury yachts and glamorous women. Now he was married to this gorgeous, fascinating woman with mesmerising eyes that seemed at certain times to be dark pools of sympathy and solicitude and others, when the sun caught them, flashing amber like those of a wildcat.

So determined was the Earl to believe he was doing the right thing that he deliberately blotted out any warning voices that might have intruded upon his honeymoon period. He chose to forget that he'd already cancelled plans for a spring wedding to Jamila as it 'didn't feel right' and he also made a conscious decision not to invite any of his family in Britain to join in the celebration: he could guess what they'd have had to say. In the past couple of years the Earl's sister Frances and two sons Anthony and Nicholas had watched him lurch from one unsuitable relationship to another with ever increasing disapproval and concern.

Anthony Ashley-Cooper winced as he remembered his previous girlfriend Nathalie Lions, the 29-year-old French lingerie model he had been involved with until recently. Of course he'd been besotted with her, who wouldn't be? In addition to the dark, exotic looks he always found such a turn-on, she'd also had a perfect figure – tiny waist and large, pneumatic breasts. So what if they were just a little bit surgically enhanced? Lots of women, particularly models, put themselves under the knife to enhance their natural assets these days; it was almost an occupational hazard.

The lovesick Earl had paraded Nathalie around in public like a new state-of-the-art sportscar. He revelled in the envious glances from other men at clubs in the south of France, London and Barbados. She made him feel young again – as if some of her youthful energy rubbed off on him the way her perfume sometimes lingered on his clothes. Anxious not to appear the frumpy sad-sap older escort, he took to wearing lurid silk shirts, leather trousers and gold chains, hoping the garish clothes would detract attention from his thinning grey hair and sagging paunch.

Whatever Nathalie wanted, he'd given her – a £100,000 Rolex watch, an Audi TT sports car. Friends and family warned him that he was turning himself into a walking chequebook for the young beauty but he was too infatuated to care. Only when a British tabloid printed revelations of Nathalie's lurid past as a Penthouse 'pet' had the Earl finally, grudgingly, parted company with his young paramour. By then he'd already lavished around £1m on her.

Hot on the heels of the Nathalie Lions débâcle, the Earl knew his impulsive marriage to Jamila wasn't exactly going to be a cause for celebration among the family back home. He didn't imagine there would be many champagne corks popping at his 9,000-acre estate in Wimborne St Giles, Dorset when news of his nuptials broke. That's why he'd kept the wedding deliberately low-key. There'd be plenty of time to prove to them that he'd got it spot on this time, that he was going to be married to Jamila for the rest of his life.

In this at least, he would be proven right. But what the Earl had no way of knowing then, as he lovingly brushed a lock of long, sun-bleached hair away from his new wife's face, was how little of that life he had left.

★ ★ ★ ★ ★

The first ten-elevenths of the 10th Earl of Shaftesbury's life was about as far removed as possible from his later decadent existence on the French Riviera. Born on 22 May 1938, Anthony Ashley-Cooper had shouldered the mantle of responsibility from an early age after his father died when he was only 8. From then on, he'd spent his time shuttling backwards and forwards between Paris – where his French mother lived – and boarding school at Eton. During his holidays he often stayed in Dorset with his grandparents, getting to know the estate he would one day inherit.

Wimborne St Giles is a sprawling estate that takes in four villages and a huge seventeenth-century family home. It is quintessentially English in the way Americans always envision English country life to be – tea and cakes in the afternoon, church fêtes on the village green and a meandering river by which to picnic on long, hot summer's days. The various Earls of Shaftesbury have overseen the estate with a generally benevolent, progressive patriarchy. The 7th Earl was a leading child labour reformer in the Victorian era and his work in making education compulsory for everyone led to him being commemorated by the statue of Eros in London's Piccadilly Circus, whose arrow points directly in the direction of Wimborne St Giles.

The motto of the Ashley family is 'Love, Serve' and for the first 60 years of his life, the 10th Earl seemed to accomplish both those things with a dutiful cheerfulness. After succeeding to the earldom on his grandfather's death in 1961, he ran the estate with efficiency and respect, earning a reputation for himself as a leading conservationist. He knew most of his residents on the estate by name and became president of the Hawk and Owl Trust and vice-president of Sir David Attenborough's Butterfly Conservation charity.

In matters of love Anthony Ashley-Cooper wove a slightly more erratic early path, however. He just wasn't attracted to the English rose debutante type whom he'd described while at Eton as 'round shouldered' and 'unsophisticated'. Instead he much preferred the dark, smouldering looks of the Mediterranean women whom he met on a skiing holiday. In 1966 he married Italian born Bianca le Vien, the former wife of an American film producer that he met on a skiing holiday. As she was a divorcee more than 10 years his senior, the marriage raised many a perfectly groomed eyebrow among the British upper classes particularly as it took place in secret without any of the groom's family present. When it ended a decade later due to his infidelity, the Earl once more became one of the most eligible men in the country, causing a flutter in the hearts of ambitious society matrons with daughters of marriageable age. His second venture into matrimony was with another divorcee: Christina Casella, the daughter of the Swedish ambassador. This marriage would last nearly a quarter of a century and would produce two male heirs, Anthony and Nicholas.

On his regular foreign jaunts Anthony enjoyed a break from stiff upper lip constraints and gave full rein to his fondness for good living and heavy drinking. Despite this, he was always careful to maintain his image at home as a committed member of the ruling elite. As the twentieth century wound to an end, it appeared the 10th Earl of Shaftesbury would live out his life in predictable respectability, carrying out his estate duties with diligence and keeping his playboy streak buried.

Some men go through a mid-life crisis in their forties or fifties when they start to question who they are, what they're doing and what direction they want their life to take. Anthony Ashley-Cooper was over 60 when the death of his beloved mother triggered a full-blown identity crisis. He was completely devastated by her death as only sons of widowed mothers often are. It made him re-evaluate everything about his life and find it all cruelly wanting. Suddenly the man he'd tried so hard to be all those years – the conscientious, conservative family man – was exposed as a sham. It was a mask he'd worn to please those around him.

The death of a parent comes as a two-pronged attack. It at once takes away the compass by which we've steered our lives up to this point and at the same time reminds us sharply of our own mortality and of the fact that life is not – as the cliché goes – a dress rehearsal. Anthony Ashley-Cooper's sister, Lady Frances, describes her brother as being left an 'orphan at the age of 61' by their mother's death. She believes it caused him to 'lose his grip on reality'.

The Earl, however, would have described it as finally facing up to a different reality – one he'd been suppressing all his life. Without his mother he felt bereft and at the same time liberated – a uniquely confusing combination of emotions. He missed her terribly but equally he felt as if a weight had been lifted off him. The burden of being the 'good son' and the 'responsible aristocrat' and of living up to expectations he now saw had been foisted on him. At an age when most people are pocketing their free bus passes and slipping quietly into retirement, Anthony Ashley-Cooper decided it was time to start again. He was going to be reborn.

The first year of the new Millennium was a tumultuous one for the 10th Earl. He divorced his wife Christina after 24 years together and moved out of the Wimborne estate, leaving the day-to-day running of the place to his son Anthony. Settling briefly in Hove, on the south coast, he embarked on the bar-hopping lifestyle that would characterise his last years, finding comfort in the kind of female company that can be bought for the price of a bottle of champagne. Drawn back to France, he acquired a luxury flat in Versailles, recreating wholesale two rooms from his late mother's house in a desperate bid to inject some familiarity and stability into his increasingly wayward life. But it was in the south of France, the playground of the idle rich, that Anthony found a place that appealed to his latent lust for glitz and glamour and his repudiation of the mundane and the middle-of-the-road, the dull and the dutiful. It would take the Earl a long time to realise that the French Riviera was just like the glitterballs that adorned the ceilings of the nightclubs he was so fond of – sparkling and seductive on the outside but at heart empty and hollow.

There was a time when Cannes and Nice attracted the crème de la crème of celebrity society drawn by the fashionable clientele of its resorts, the dramatic rocky coastline and the legend that had built up over the years. There was a decadent social scene where Europe's beautiful people partied away against a backdrop of the crystal blue Mediterranean. By the time the 10th Earl of Shaftesbury became a fixture at the clubs and bars here, however, the whiff of glamour had been largely overpowered by the stench of corruption.

Where once A-list film stars, writers and painters had walked bare foot along the beaches and danced al fresco on sultry summer nights, now the Côte d'Azur played host to a very different type of visitor. Organised gangs from Russia and North Africa now worked and played in the streets and squares stars such as Brigitte Bardot had once made their own. Around themselves they built up a seedy underworld of shady clubs and high- (and not so high) class prostitution. These were the kind of places where money can buy you anything – from a conversation to a private dance – and lonely old men with pockets deep enough to fork out £30 on a glass of bubbly can find plenty of willing company.

This was where Anthony Ashley-Cooper gravitated during the loose, lost years following his mother's death. Several nights a week, the 6ft Earl, wearing one of his distinctive outfits often teamed with outsized red and black glasses, would knock on the metal grill of one of the private members clubs and burst in, introducing himself with the words: 'I'm the Earl of Shaftesbury. I'm a millionaire.' Not surprisingly Anthony never lacked company for his forays into the Côte d'Azur's shadowy underworld where he became known simply as 'The Count'. There was always a steady stream of attractive young women happy to hang on his arm in exchange for money or jewellery, or trips to exotic locations.

While he loved the variety and the excitement of having lots of different women around him, the Count missed the comfort he'd enjoyed during his marriage: the feeling that there was someone there to come home to, to look out for him and to look after him. So when he met Jamila M'Barek she seemed like the answer to his prayers. Glamorous and attractive, and no stranger to the hostess bars he so loved, she appealed to his newly awakened wild side. As a mother of two, however, she also had a nurturing streak that gave him hope that he might once again be cared for, as he had been when his mother was alive.

'You're wonderful,' he'd murmur into her ear. 'I don't want to be without you.' But Jamila M'Barek had more pressing things on her mind than taking care of an ageing, alcohol-sozzled admirer. Growing up one of seven children of an abusive father, she'd learned young that life didn't always offer up its bounty on a plate and that sometimes you had to do things you might not choose to in order to ultimately get what you want. In Jamila's world, the end almost always justified the means. Like all of us, she was looking for love but for her love had become inextricably linked with money. It was a dangerous misconception.

Although her former husband – a Dutch millionaire – left her pretty well provided for, Jamila wanted more. She craved financial security and relished the finer things in life but seemed to lack the strong will and self-discipline needed to carve out a career for herself. Instead she relied on her greatest asset: her own physical charm. While her children were mostly cared for by their grandparents, Jamila had plenty of time to focus on herself, making sure her hair and clothes were perfect, watching and waiting for someone or something to come along and provide her with the life she believed she deserved. As she approached 40, often finding herself surrounded in the hostess bars by women half her age, Jamila must have known that her window of opportunity was closing fast. The Earl of Shaftesbury was just what she needed.

Who knows what unspoken pact was reached when Jamila and Anthony Ashley-Cooper decided to get married. Was he, weakened by the effects of alcohol abuse and age, looking for a glamorous carer who'd slip effortlessly in and out of her dual bedroom roles as sex-provider and nursemaid? And was she, ever conscious of the ticking of the clock, resigned to trading sex for material comfort and a secure future? Or was there a genuine affection between these two mismatched and ultimately lonely people? Was there a real shared vision of a future in which they helped and supported each other, steering one another through the under-lit, seedy night-time world they'd both come to know so well?

At the beginning at least, the Earl was certainly besotted with his new bride – Madame La Comptesse as he liked her to be called – and she indulgent with him as with a misbehaving child who can't really be held responsible for his actions. But the honeymoon period lasted barely as long as the gaps between Jamila's nail treatments.

'He's always taking Viagra and having testosterone injections and then wanting sex in the middle of the night,' Jamila would complain to her sisters. Her new husband's family were equally unimpressed with his choice of bride. Lady Frances, who met her new sister-in-law only once soon after the wedding, found her to be 'cunning' and 'calculating'.

Anthony bought his wife a sumptuous £500,000 apartment in a converted Normandy-style house in the desirable La Californie area of Cannes, an exclusive hilly enclave of multi-million pound villas, but he himself spent less and less time there. Jamila was always griping about something or so it seemed. At the start she'd seemed so happy to take care of him but now she just got irritated with everything he did. She spent hours on the phone disparaging him to her sisters or to her younger brother Mohamed. And who wanted to make love to a woman who reacted to his advances with a look of mild disgust? Especially when there were plenty of other younger, prettier girls more than willing to take her place.

The Earl had his own house in Antibes, a favourite holiday hangout of the international yachting set, and conveniently placed between Nice and Cannes. Increasingly, he began to leave Jamila to her own devices in the Californie flat, preferring the company of other hostesses who didn't complain about his heavy drinking or sexual demands. After feeling like he'd missed out on his youth due to the burden of family responsibility, all he really wanted as his early 60s gave way to his mid-60s was an easy life. Jamila wasn't about to give him that, however.

There are people who are prepared to work at their relationships when they start going wrong and then there are others who decide to cut their losses and run. In later life Anthony Ashley-Cooper definitely fell into the second camp. The problem was that there were just so many women and so little time. Why would he want to get bogged down trying to please a wife who just seemed to find fault with everything he did?

As his domestic affairs became increasingly tense, the Earl's drinking – always prodigious – stepped up a gear and there were always plenty of liggers at the hostess bars he frequented who were more than happy to take advantage of the drunken aristocrat's legendary booze-induced generosity. Jamila would later claim to have come back to her flat one night to find two strange women helping themselves to her belongings while her husband slumped nearby in an alcoholic stupor.

By spring 2004 it was clear that the marriage had run its course. The Earl knew he'd made a mistake but, true to form, he wasn't about to sit around moping over what might have been or to throw himself into an intensive round of therapy to try and work out what might have gone wrong. Instead he just wanted to move on. Jamila, however, wasn't going to rush things. The relationship might be on the rocks but she wasn't about to bail out completely without having all her financial bases covered. Unlike her wandering husband, Jamila had looked at life from both sides of the poverty line and she knew which she preferred. Typically, her close-knit family gathered around her to offer advice on how to ensure she got the best possible outcome in any divorce settlement. Particularly vocal with his suggestions was factory-worker Mohamed, currently living with his second wife in Munich.

At the time of their separation, Jamila's 18-month marriage to the Earl netted her the flat in Cannes, a windmill in a different region of France, a top-of-the-range 4x4 car and a monthly allowance of around 10,000 euros. But what would a divorce court make of the arrangements? Might she be entitled to an even larger slice of the Ashley family pie or would her generous allowance be slashed instead? Jamila knew she was walking a legal and financial tightrope. The 10th Earl of Shaftesbury wasn't going to let niggling worries about money intrude in his hedonistic lifestyle. After his separation from Jamila, he continued his nocturnal habits and eventually hooked up with another hostess, this time a Moroccan woman called

Nadia, who was at that time in her early thirties. Before long he'd set her and her two children up in their own flat and was promising to make her his fourth wife. All he had to do was just sort out this bothersome business of the divorce from Jamila.

On 3 November 2004 Anthony Ashley-Cooper flew into the Riviera after telling his eldest son that he was going to sort things out with Jamila once and for all. The Earl was in good humour. He always loved being in Cannes, with its grand architecture and designer shops... and of course, its seedy bars where he'd become such a familiar figure. Free from obligations and expectations, he felt at home there. Booking himself into the Noga Hilton, a luxury hotel right on the seafront and just a short walk from his favourite regular haunts, he breathed in the fresh sea air. November in the south of France can be bitterly cold, with the savage Mistral wind blowing in from the north, but Anthony didn't mind the chill. In a strange way it reminded him of Dorset and besides, it was amazing how a few stiff vodkas could take the edge off the cold.

His new girlfriend Nadia was at first delighted to have the generous Earl back again, but she soon grew fed up when she realised that he had other ideas for celebrating his first few days back in France rather than cosy nights in with her and her children. 'What do you have to go out drinking for?' she yelled at him. 'Why do you need to talk to women in bars when you've got me here? If you go out, we're finished!' But to the Earl, frequenting seedy hostess bars and clubs had become a natural part of life in France. He simply wasn't prepared to compromise the freedom that had come to him so late in life.

On the evening of 5 November, while his family and tenants back home were celebrating Guy Fawkes night, the Earl set off as usual to see whether he could find any fireworks of his own in the side street dive bars. Bar staff recall the gangly Peer seemed perhaps a little less exuberant than normal, but he still chatted to a few of the hostesses in his eccentric, charming manner and downed several large drinks. Perhaps the 66-year-old Lord was upset after a quarrel with his latest lady friend, they speculated, or just a little tired. No doubt he'd be back to his usual form as soon as he'd had a chance to readjust to the strange hours demanded by nocturnal Riviera life.

But Anthony Ashley-Cooper never did get a chance to hold court once again in the seedy basement bars and clubs the Cannes tourist board never sees fit to mention. After 5 November, the flamboyant Earl quite simply disappeared. Used to hearing from him every few days, his family started to compulsively re-check their answer-phone messages, wondering if there was something they'd missed. Friends he'd been due to meet up with became uneasy about his uncharacteristic silence. Sure, it was possible he had decided on a whim to jet off somewhere – he'd occasionally done such things before when pressures got too much for him –but never without letting anyone know where he was.

As days went into weeks and still no contact, the mystery of 'Le Lord disparu' intensified. His mobile phone was dead and someone had withdrawn £200 cash with his Barclaycard but it wasn't clear who it was, or where this had occurred. Rumours began circulating through the back streets of southern France's ritziest resorts. Le Compt had serious money troubles, he'd been conned by an underworld gang who had stolen a valuable painting from his Versailles flat, he'd been kidnapped, he'd jumped off a cliff into the sea… It seemed everyone had a theory about what had happened to the man his lawyer described as 'likeable and generous but also weak and fragile.'

As time went on with still no word, any innocent explanations were reluctantly ruled out and foul play now seemed to be the only reasonable assumption. To his family's horror, by December 2004, the French police were treating Anthony Ashley-Cooper's disappearance as a murder inquiry.

Now the rumour mill really went into overdrive. Owing to his penchant for sleazy bars, the Earl had been involved with some very shady people in recent years. With the kind of company he'd been keeping, who knew what could have happened to him? Vice rings, Mafia gangs – anything was possible on the Côte d'Azur.

The increasingly fanciful speculation finally ended on 25

February 2005 with the dramatic news that Jamila – the Earl's former wife in his third and shortest-lived marriage – had been arrested by French police. The following day her brother Mohamed was also arrested and they were being investigated for murder.

Over the next days and weeks, a broken, desperate Jamila admitted she had been involved in her husband's death. He'd come to the flat to talk to her about money, she told police. They were trying to iron out details of the divorce settlement in which she hoped to receive several hundred thousand pounds. Her brother Mohamed happened to be there as well on that day and he'd joined in the discussions, trying, she claimed, to look out for his sister's interests.

As so often happens when money becomes an issue in the wake of a recent marriage break-up, the conversation soon became heated. Jamila claimed both her husband and brother had been drinking heavily and eventually the combination of alcohol and dissent erupted into a blazing row during which her brother unintentionally bludgeoned her husband to death. Afterwards Mohamed panicked and bundled the Earl's body into the boot of his car before driving off alone to dispose of it. Jamila had been an emotional wreck ever since, she said, and had been receiving treatment for depression.

On 5 April 2005 the remains of a body were found in the Vallon de la Rague, 10km west of Cannes. This hidden gully above a luxury marina, where a stream wends its way through the rocks towards the sea, is used mostly by lone middle-aged Scandinavian hikers or by joggers looking for a more challenging run. On this particular day, however, police – acting on information they'd been given – swarmed the rubbish-strewn beauty spot and eventually found what they were looking for hidden under a laurel tree.

Days later, DNA tests confirmed the skeletal remains were those of Le Lord disparu: the 10th Earl of Shaftesbury. The Ashley family was devastated. The Earl's eccentricities hadn't stopped him being well loved. And the family's grief was compounded still further when, just six weeks after the Earl's body was discovered, his eldest son died of a heart attack at the age of just 27.

In a hearing in France in September 2005 Mohamed M'Barek admitted accidentally killing his brother-in-law and disposing of the body but claimed it was not premeditated and that his sister had no part in it. It had been a drunken brawl, he said. He hadn't intended to hurt anyone; it was just a tragic accident.

The French authorities weren't convinced. On 25 May 2007, a Nice court found Jamila and Mohamed guilty of murder and sentenced them each to 25 years in jail. The court had heard that Jamila had paid her brother £105,000 to kill her husband because she feared losing out financially in a divorce settlement.

'It further confirms the type of people we thought they were,' said the Earl's son Nicholas after the verdict. 'Cold, deceitful and without compassion for a man they murdered and betrayed.'

The Earl is buried alongside his eldest son in the family vault of the church at Wimborne, St Giles. Steeped in history, the weathered grey stone church looks serenely out across the village green. It's a long way from the back streets of Cannes, where a man can spend his life lurching from one dimly lit bar to the next and never see the fabled Riviera sun.

It was the search for love that led the 10th Earl of Shaftesbury to explore the seedier side of life in the south of France. He thought that love could be bought for the price of a high-class cocktail but in the end he paid heavily for his own mistake.

CHAPTER SIX

'MOM, YOU'RE THE EMBODIMENT OF EVIL!'

Everyone who's ever had teenage children knows their behaviour can be erratic to say the least – polite and friendly one minute, rude and unresponsive the next. But when 15-year-old Susan Bolling, who'd always been such a conscientious student, suddenly started missing classes and making strange claims about her parents, the school counsellor at Clayton Valley High School in Concord, California worried there might be something deeper going on than just the usual adolescent angst.

It was 1972 and psychotherapy was just starting to become the nation's favourite pastime, particularly in trendy California. The pretty, slim teen's parents had just got divorced and the counsellor thought she might benefit from some more intensive therapy. 'It might help for her to talk to someone who specialises in adolescent behaviour,' Susan's mother, Helen, was told. The counsellor recommended Dr Felix Polk, a psychologist who had gained an excellent reputation locally for dealing with troubled teens.

At this time Felix Polk was 40 years old and married with two children. Born into a wealthy Jewish Austrian family, his childhood had been shattered when the Holocaust forced his family to flee. But his traumatic early life had done little to diminish his appreciation for life and culture and art. According to his many admirers, Felix was the kind of man who always saw the good in everything; he embraced new experiences and exuded passion. He was, they all agreed, tremendously enriching company.

With curly brown hair, a high forehead, sensual mouth and hooded eyes that burned with intellectual intensity, handsome Felix cut an attractive figure. Helen Bolling was immediately won over. 'I'm sure he'll be able to help you,' she told her surly, defensive daughter. Privately, she was concerned that Susan would take against the urbane, confident psychologist. After all, she'd been so contrary recently, so difficult to reach. This was the girl who preferred to spend her weekends reading weighty Russian novels engaging in dark themes of death, guilt, longing and futility rather than to go shopping with friends as her classmates seemed to do. She was also known for her sudden flares of temper and quicksilver mood changes. Who knew how she'd react?

When Susan and Felix clicked, practically right from the word go, Helen was overjoyed. Susan needed a reliable father figure that she could look up to and be guided by. It was such a relief that she'd found someone she could confide in. However, it was only after a good few private sessions with Felix Polk that Susan said something to her mother that made the older woman's blood freeze within her chest. 'She said something about sitting on his lap,' Helen would later recall.

Put yourself in Helen Bolling's position at this point. Here's this troubled teenager – your daughter – who's been becoming increasingly withdrawn from you but then finally, thankfully, you've found somebody who can reach her. You've invested your hopes in this person who comes highly recommended by all the authorities and believe they can help sort out your daughter's problems and keep her from going further off the rails. Then something gets said that sets off maternal alarm bells. Are you over-reacting? Your daughter seems well and happy and, moreover, is making good progress. And this other person is an experienced professional, an expert in his field who has worked with hundreds of other adolescents. Would you stick your neck out and make a fuss, perhaps jeopardising the very progress your daughter has already made?

Despite her very real reservations, Helen Bolling decided

not to report Felix to the authorities. 'Maybe that's the way they do things now,' she said. Even in her own head, she could hear how weak that explanation sounded. She confronted Felix, telling him the inappropriate behaviour had to stop, but she decided not to take the matter any further. She had no idea how bitterly she'd come to regret that decision.

Helen Bolling would later claim that Dr Felix Polk – eminent psychologist and 40-year-old father-of-two – used those sessions to hypnotise or drug her daughter before having sex with her. Could that be true? Of course, his supporters vehemently deny it. What seems clear is that the relationship formed during those sessions went far and beyond a legitimate therapist–client bond. This was so much so that even when the young Susan Bolling stopped her counselling sessions she carried on seeing Felix Polk despite the fact that he was married and more than twice her age.

There's a recognised syndrome where vulnerable patients or clients fall in love with the professional who's been giving them advice or counselling, whether it's a doctor, lawyer, teacher … or psychologist. But what happened between Susan and Felix was reciprocal. It wasn't an impressionable teenager fixating on her glamorous older therapist, but a mutual passion and one which, given Felix's status and position, was at best inappropriate and at worst deeply immoral.

If Helen Bolling had hoped that going away to college would cure her wayward daughter of any feelings for Felix

Polk, she was sadly disappointed. Susan went to Mills College and then onto San Fransisco State University to study literature. Instead of the experience making her realise how much more fun it was to hang out with people her own age she just found her peers shallow and unsophisticated in comparison with her older, well-travelled lover.

She did try to break it off once, however. 'I don't want to be with you anymore,' she told Felix, only to retract it almost immediately when she heard how broken he was. Listening to him sobbing because she was threatening to leave him gave Susan a little thrill of power. Sure, he might have all the qualifications and the success and the big career but she was the one in control. What Susan didn't consider then was that maybe, just maybe, Felix was giving her the illusion of control and these tears were just another way of manipulating her and keeping her where he wanted her.

Nearly a decade passed and Susan and Felix's illicit relationship had already lasted longer than many marriages. Clearly this wasn't some schoolgirl crush that was just going to 'fizzle out'. Finally Felix Polk divorced his first wife Sharon, the mother of his son and daughter. This left him free to marry Susan. The wedding in 1982 evoked mixed feelings in most of the guests. On the one hand the couple looked genuinely in love. Susan, slim and lovely with a garland of white flowers nestling in her cloud of dark hair, giggled with girlish delight while cutting the cake as her debonair, rugged-looking husband gazed indulgently on. After all those years, they seemed so at ease with each other, so comfortable in each other's presence.

On the other hand there was the age gap. At 25 years, it was simply too great to ignore. 50-year-old Felix could just as well have been giving 25-year-old Susan away as making her his wife. What were the chances of such a relationship working out? In 20 years' time he'd be an old man while she'd still be in the prime of life. And wasn't there just a little touch of the Svengalis about how he treated her? Wouldn't she end up resenting being constantly in his shadow? Not that everyone didn't wish the happy couple well but more than one wedding guest went home with a lurking suspicion that this marriage would end badly. What they could never have imagined was just how badly.

For a long while after the Polks' wedding, it seemed as if the doubters were to be proved wrong. Felix went on consolidating his professional reputation as a psychologist, specialising in disturbed children and adolescents. He built up an impressive private practice in Berkeley, which was a mecca for liberal intellectuals, and, by the late eighties he had also added teaching and lecturing to his already heavy workload. Colleagues and patients were won over by his sensitivity when dealing with patients who were often traumatised, as well as his intuitive understanding of complex emotional problems. Susan, meanwhile, had three sons – Adam, Eli and Gabriel – in close succession and threw herself into motherhood with the same intense passion with which she did everything else in her life. She, and her husband when he was home, spent a lot of time ferrying their boys around to baseball games and football matches.

As Felix's professional stature grew, so too did the family's standard of living. They travelled extensively, drove stylish cars and the boys attended the best schools. By the time they'd been married 18 years, they'd bought their dream home — a spacious, wood-clad house in the leafy town of Orinda, nestling in the Oakland Hills. For the West Coast's chattering classes Orinda is a suburban paradise. An easy commute from San Francisco or Oakland, it is characterised by the kind of individual, distinctive houses you normally see gracing the pages of *Architectural Review*, and all set against a breathtaking backdrop of rolling green hills and spreading oak trees.

The Polk's house on Miner Road was situated in its own compound complete with multi-levelled, wood-decked terraces and a separate cottage by the swimming pool. Although the house was hugely expensive, there was nothing in the least bit bling about it. From the polished hardwood floors scattered with warm-coloured rugs to the exposed stone fireplace in the living room, everything was tasteful and subtle. The big picture windows looked out onto the surrounding woods where beautiful mossy-trunked trees formed a canopy of greenery that shielded the compound from the harsh Californian sun, throwing dappled shadows onto the natural brick steps and weathered wooden decks. But although everything outside the Orinda house was peace and tranquillity, inside the atmosphere was anything but.

While the Polks had steadily wrapped themselves in a mink-lined cocoon of luxury and status, their marriage had been busily unravelling from within. Susan Polk had always had a temper. She was quick to lash out when something annoyed her. Sometimes she'd fly off the handle when there didn't seem to be any good reason for it. And Felix wasn't the type of man who'd back down on an argument. At times he would deliberately goad his wife, calling her 'crazy', trying to verbally wrong-foot her. As with so many warring couples, it was the children who'd invariably end up in the middle. 'Please stop it,' they would entreat. 'Can't we all just get on?'

But when a couple falls into a pattern of accusations and recriminations, of attack and counter-attack, it becomes very difficult to break that pattern even when those getting hurt are the very people you most want to protect. Susan would tell people later that Felix had routinely emotionally and physically abused her and the children, that he'd tried to control her life so that she was cut off from friends and family and had no chance of developing a support network. Helen Bolling, Susan's mother, later lent credence to that particular suggestion when she claimed Felix had systematically excluded her from family life, making it clear that he didn't want her around. Susan accused him of threatening to kill her and himself, the boys and even the dogs if she ever tried to leave him. For his part, Felix would imply that Susan was emotionally disturbed and that it was she herself who was threatening him with violence. He branded her 'delusional' and claimed that she invented situations that didn't exist and memories of events that never happened.

At one point Susan claimed to have recovered memories of childhood abuse – a claim that was strongly denied. Both the Polks also accused their son Adam's day-care centre of ritualistic satanic abuse although no evidence was ever found (later, a babysitter also came under suspicion of abuse).

So what was it all about, this attention-seeking marriage? Were the Polks somehow addicted to the drama of it all, unable to cope with the routine of life without an injection of controversy? Did they manufacture confrontation – with each other or the outside world – as a way of getting through the tawdry ordinariness of suburban life? Whatever the truth, neighbours in the upscale Orinda community caught the whiff of dysfunction that wafted down from the Polk compound. They became wary of the volatile couple, reluctant to get too close to them and particularly to Susan, who had a reputation for being nervy and quick to take offence.

As the new Millennium got underway with all its promise of a shiny new beginning, the Polks' relationship started to nosedive out of control. Susan's eccentric ideas, her 'delusions' as her denigrating husband insisted on calling them, became more extreme. She claimed to be psychic and to have predicted the 9/11 attacks. Not only this but she also became convinced Felix was actually an agent from the Israeli Secret Police and was passing on her psychic predictions to Mossad. One of her other recurring themes was that Felix was amassing a huge fortune stashed away in secret Cayman Island bank accounts. 'Your Mom's crazy,' Felix would tell his sons, shaking his head in disbelief.

For the three Polk boys, it was like living in a war zone. Each parent began to accuse the other of physical violence and would claim that the other was trying to control their lives. Always slim, Susan now began to look positively gaunt. Happy to play the martyr in family conflicts, she used her physical frailty to back up assertions that it was she and not Felix, who was the victim of domestic violence. In January 2001 she attempted suicide, claiming Felix's physical and mental cruelty had driven her over the edge.

Several times the police were called out to the $1.85m Orinda property, with its classy wooden balustrades and exposed wooden rafters, to deal with allegations of assault from one or other of the Polk parents. No wonder the three boys began to self-destruct, the two younger ones in particular playing up at school and getting into trouble with the authorities.

By late 2001 it was obvious that the long-lived marriage had become too toxic to be anything but doomed and Susan Polk decided to file for divorce. You'd think a well-off

Above: Rena Salmon, who brutally blasted her husband Paul's new lover, Lorna Stewart *(above right),* twice with a shotgun while she was at work in her beauty salon.

Barton Corbin, the respected community dentist from a seemingly perfect all-American family, finally shows his true colours as he confesses to murdering his wife Jennifer in 2004 and fellow dentistry student Dolly Hearn in 1990.

Inset: A distraught Heather Tierney holding up pictures of her murdered sister, Jennifer Corbin, to the media.
© *PA Photos*

Gary Malone making a bogus TV appeal for information about the whereabouts of his wife Sharon (*inset*). He knew full well her body was lying in Hertfordshire woodland where he dumped it after bludgeoning her to death.

© *PA Photos*

Anthony Ashley-Cooper, 10th Earl of Shaftesbury, with his then wife
Jamila M'Barek.   © *Reuters*

Susan Polk – 'the embodiment of evil' – killed her husband after eighteen years of marriage.

Above: The Pemberton family: (*from left to right*) Laura, William, Julia and Alan. On Tuesday, 18 November 2003, Alan, a psychotic and obsessive father and husband, callously gunned down his estranged wife Julia and their seventeen-year-old son William before turning the gun on himself and taking his own life.

Below left: Quiet, good-natured Toby Charnaud, who'd never hurt anyone, had his life ended in the most brutal and shocking way possible.

On 6 September 2006, Pannada Charnaud was found guilty of the murder of her ex-husband Toby Charnaud (*previous page*) and, along with the three men she'd hired to carry out the killing, was sentenced to life imprisonment.

© *PA Photos*

Derek Symmons attacked and beat Christine *(inset)*, his wife of thirty-eight years, to death, then he bundled her into the boot of his car and drove to the south of France.

© *PA Photos*

couple who by this stage couldn't stand the sight of each other, who were turning their home into an emotional bloodbath that their children were forced to witness, might opt for a clean break – but not the Polks. In a disastrous decision they decided to live separately under the same roof while details of the divorce settlement were thrashed out.

Of course, there are various practical reasons why they may have chosen to remain on the same property even after separating. For a start there was the question of who would get possession of the house itself, the material embodiment of all their early aspirations, the dream home that had so quickly become the setting for a living nightmare. Then there were the children. By this time Adam and Eli were pretty independent but Gabriel was still just 14. Who would get custody? He was already showing signs of being emotionally disturbed by the turbulence in the household and each parent considered themselves better equipped to offer a steadying influence than the other. As an interim measure Felix was ordered to pay Susan $6,500 per month in maintenance, a crippling financial burden for the nearly 70-year-old psychologist. 'You can afford it,' Susan would jeer at him. 'I know you've got millions secretly hidden away.'

It was around this time that the last vestiges of the façade of domestic harmony that the Polks had tried to present to colleagues and the local community finally crumbled away. Felix confided in friends that Susan had started to walk around the house with a gun and he was terrified of what she meant to do with it. 'I have to barricade myself into my room,' he told them. On one occasion when the police were called to the house, in a fit of uncontrollable anger Susan hit her husband in front of them and was taken to the police station. Felix refused to press charges, however.

Susan took to openly discussing how she might kill her husband. 'Hmm, I wonder if I'd be better off shooting him or drowning him. Or maybe I should just tamper with his car,' she'd muse to Gabriel as if she was debating what to cook for dinner.

It was a blessed relief when Susan announced that she was considering moving to Montana. Over the course of 2002 she spent considerable periods of time scouring the area, looking for the best place to live, the best schools. If she moved away, then at least the bitterness would stop, her friends and family reasoned. With a bit of distance between them, perhaps the Polks could actually come to some sort of truce and start to introduce some sense of stability into the lives of their increasingly troubled sons.

In the autumn of 2002 Susan was once again back in Montana laying down the groundwork for her eventual move. With Susan gone – even briefly – the Orinda house finally became what it had never really been – a home. Felix Polk loved the uncustomary calmness. He relished waking up in the mornings to see the weak autumn sun dancing across the deck and hearing the gentle sway of trees in the breeze. Now he looked forward to gazing out the picture windows as the sun set and soaking in the sheer beauty of the surrounding scenery. Finally he had some time to contemplate the mess he and Susan had made of their marriage and how it had affected his sons. Being the youngest, Gabriel weighed particularly on his mind. Recently he had been going increasingly off the rails, prompting bitter clashes between father and son.

'Both you and Eli seem to have bought into Mom's horror stories about me,' Felix wrote in a letter to his youngest son at the start of the summer. 'They are for the most part not true stories but I don't really have a chance to speak up for myself. I am faced with a closed system in which Mom says what she says so hatefully about me and I have no chance to point out what is true and what is not. I fear you have joined Mom who at times – and certainly about me – has created a reality of her own. I have some real flaws and yet I am not the monster she portrays me to be… I want you to know that I plan to stay around and not go away from you. You are my kid and I love you as fully as I can love anyone.'

Eli had already given Felix enough to worry about. He was presently in juvenile detention following a nasty fistfight. Felix was anxious Gabriel shouldn't end up there as well. More than ever he was more convinced Gabriel needed some fair but firm – and above all, consistent – parenting. And he was unlikely to get that from his mother. Secretly Felix had filed an application for custody of Gabriel plus full possession of the home. But what Felix Polk didn't realise was that by filing that divorce application, he would effectively be signing his own death warrant.

When Susan heard what Felix had done, she was outraged. 'I'm coming back now to sort this out!' she stormed. Knowing how volatile his wife had been over the last few months, Felix was seriously alarmed. 'She says she's bought a shotgun,' he told worried friends.

When Susan returned to the Miner Road house, she was blazing with fury. If Felix thought he was going to kick her out of her own home he had another thing coming. On 10 October 2002, as soon as Felix was out of the house she had the locks changed and moved his belongings out of the main house and into the tiny guesthouse by the pool on the lower level of the compound. 'Don't do this,' Gabreil pleaded, as his mother lugged his father's bedding down the stairs. But Susan wouldn't listen.

When Felix got back he called the police. He knew Susan wasn't legally entitled to turn him out, but he didn't know what he could do about it. Increasingly in fear of his life, he asked officers to stay while he collected some more of his stuff from the main house. He and Gabriel then left to spend the night in a hotel.

The next day the police were again called to find Felix brandishing a court order. It was proof that his divorce application had been granted. He had exclusive control of the house and custody of Gabriel, now 15. Felix's monthly payments to Susan were also drastically cut to $1,700 per month. The authorities' view was that Susan was a well-educated 44-year-old so there was no reason why she couldn't earn her own living rather than relying on her 70-year-old husband.

Now that he had the written evidence of his entitlement, Felix wanted the police to force Susan out of the house but wavered when he was told that a citizens arrest was the only way of getting her to leave if she refused to do so. Angry and scared, the 70-year-old retreated back to the pool house to try to think what to do next. Susan, of course, was seething with anger. She couldn't believe Felix had gone behind her back to take from her the most precious things in her life – her children and her home. How dare he try to manipulate her like that? He'd soon find out that she was no longer merely a patient to be pushed around. And in getting involved with his teenaged patient three decades before, like Frankenstein before him, Dr Felix Polk had created a monster – and now the monster was fighting back.

On 13 October, Felix Polk dropped his 22-year-old son Adam off at UCLA, where he was a student, and then drove back to Orinda with Gabriel, arriving home late at night. Susan had spent the evening pacing the hardwood floors and stewing over the unfairness of the latest court order. She was convinced that this was yet another example of her husband's overwhelming need to control her and to show her that he still had power over her. Also to prove that she couldn't function effectively without him – he was pulling her strings just as he always had since she was his 15-year-old schoolgirl patient, Susan fumed. It had taken her over 20 years to get up the courage to leave him and now he was determined to make her pay by taking away her home and, she had no doubt, by turning her boys against her too.

The middle-aged, twig-thin mother pushed back her now steely grey hair and folded her arms over her bony body, rocking slightly in the armchair by the fire as she waited for her husband to return home. She was determined to confront him. He had to realise she wasn't that child-bride he'd married any more. She wasn't going to give up everything without a fight. After the hell her marriage had been for the last few years, did Felix really think she was going to agree to walk away with nothing to show for it? It astonished her that even after all this time her husband obviously didn't know her very well. Which is, after all, the tragedy of many marriage break-ups – that the intimacy and familiarity we once took for granted turns out to be an illusion that fades to nothing in the time it takes for the ink to dry on the divorce papers.

When Felix eventually arrived home – going straight down to the pool house – Susan followed him with the intent of having the whole divorce settlement issue out with him. 'Not now, I'm tired,' Felix told her, not relishing the prospect of yet another confrontation with his brittle, belligerent wife. 'Another time.' Though Susan went away, now she was even madder. What an underhand coward, she thought to herself. He tries to manipulate the system against me and now he hasn't even got the guts to talk to me about it face to face. The unfairness of it all was eating into her, so much so that she couldn't think of anything else. There was the cut in her monthly income, the fact that he was trying to take the house away from her, the way he was poisoning Gabriel against her – it all went round and round in her head until she couldn't take any more. An hour and a half after her first attempt to talk to Felix, Susan was heading back down to the pool house.

As she made her way down the natural brick steps slippery in places by cushions of green moss, Susan Polk was still seething. It was as if the momentum of her anger itself was carrying her down the stairs. How dare he think he could get away with this! How dare he! Wearing only black underpants, Felix Polk was reading when his wife came storming back to discuss their divorce. How his heart must have sunk when he heard her approach, knowing he was in for a major scene. Couldn't it at least wait for the morning, for goodness sake? He was tired and had an early start.

But Susan couldn't wait. What happened when she finally stepped through the door of that poolside cottage to confront the husband she believed was trying to break her emotionally and rob her of what she was entitled to? Only two people know for sure – and one of them is dead. The incontrovertible facts are these. There was an argument that quickly escalated into violence. During the altercation, a kitchen knife – a paring knife that was later described as the family's 'favourite' – was picked up and Susan used it to stab her husband several times. He was left for dead and lay face up in a pool of his own blood.

Susan later claimed to have acted in self-defence. She said Felix attacked her and then become enraged when she sprayed pepper into his eyes and picked up a knife. While he had her pinned down to the ground and was about to plunge the knife into her, she managed to kick him in the groin and to take the knife away from him. When he tried to take it back, biting her hand, she reached round him to stab the knife repeatedly into his side. According to Susan, after this Felix Polk – renowned psychologist, father and husband –struggled to rise to his feet. 'Oh my God, I think I'm dead!' he'd said. And then he was.

Felix Polk's supporters offered a different version of events. Susan Polk had gone down to that pool house with vengeance on her mind, they asserted. She couldn't believe her husband had gone behind her back to get custody of Gabriel and ownership of the house, and she wanted her share in the millions she thought he had squirreled away. Either she'd had the knife with her all the time, or she'd picked it up when the discussion became heated. One thing was for sure, the supporters maintained – Susan deliberately and callously stabbed her 70-year-old husband to death in a final act of cruel rage. Either way, the end result was the same. Felix Polk was dead

What went through Susan Polk's mind as she gazed down at the lifeless body of the man who'd shaped her life since she was a troubled 15-year-old? Did she think back to happier times they'd shared? Did she see the face of a husband and a father, or just a man she'd come to hate? Whatever thoughts came crowding into her mind, she managed to push them aside enough to stumble out of the pool house and back upstairs. She knew that if she called the police then her life would be over. What was the harming in waiting, she asked herself. Why rush headlong into the hell that was surely coming? Back upstairs, she cleaned the blood off the knife before replacing it carefully in the kitchen drawer. Then she washed her clothes and had a series of showers. Afterwards, incredibly, she went to bed.

It's a curious thing, the body's instinctive need to cling to routine and familiarity at times of crisis. It's as if we try to fool ourselves that doing normal things will somehow make our lives normal again. At times of unbearable turmoil, we take comfort from the mundane, the everyday. Susan Polk – who'd craved drama so much she'd previously tried to manufacture it in the accusations of child abuse, the psychic delusions – knew that what she'd done that night catapulted her into a future where nothing would ever be the same. How appealing must her dysfunctional, but safe family life have appeared at that moment as she gazed back at it from across the chasm created by killing Felix.

There are some things that, once done, can never be undone.

The next day, 14 October 2002, Susan carried on with the charade of daily life, much as though nothing had happened. In the morning, she took Gabriel to school as normal, returning to the house to find her pet Labrador, Dusty, had gone missing. She spent the day looking for Dusty, cooking and cleaning. Then she picked Gabriel up from school and took him out to lunch, dropping in at her local Blockbuster store to rent the movie *Scooby Doo* before coming home once more. It was an ordinary weekday in the life of an ordinary housewife.

As she swept floors and put out Dusty's food, did Susan think about the body lying just yards from the front door? Or did she block it out? After all, it was beyond ludicrous to imagine Felix lying down there on the stone floor in a pool of his own blood. It was simply unimaginable.

Towards the evening Gabriel Polk started to get agitated. That night his father had promised to take him to a San Francisco Giants baseball game but hadn't shown up. Susan had already moved Felix's Saab to the train station so that Gabriel wouldn't suspect anything and the boy was used to his father being out during the day but it was still unlike him to have forgotten something like this.

'Have you seen Dad?' he asked Susan.

His mother's eyelids fluttered a little as they did when she was uneasy about something, but she replied 'No.' Over the next couple of hours Gabriel would repeat the question several times but still he got the same response. One time Susan even suggested that he might ring the road traffic authorities if he was worried to check there hadn't been an accident.

Gabriel went down to the pool house but found the door locked. So his father must be out after all… and yet there was something that still didn't seem right about the whole situation, something that gave him a kind of sick feeling in his stomach. Again he went to find his mum to ask if there was any explanation she could think of for Felix's continued absence.

Then Susan said a strange thing. 'Aren't you happy he's gone?' she asked her son.

'No,' he replied.

'I am,' was her reply.

Even more unnerving was her next statement: 'I guess I didn't use a shotgun.' Even for a teenager used to hearing bizarre statements from his mother, this was disturbing.

Gabriel tried to put the gnawing worry out of his head and started playing a video game in his room. But it was no good – he just knew something was horribly wrong. With an increasing feeling of foreboding, the 15-year-old grabbed a flashlight and made his way down to the pool house, unknowingly retracing the same path his mother had taken the previous night.

Finding the front door still locked, he went in through a side entrance. What he saw will be forever imprinted on his memory: there was his father – dead. Shaking, Gabriel retreated from the pool house and made his way back up the stairs. Surely this wasn't real? It couldn't really be happening, could it? His heart was thumping as he went into the main house and took the portable phone off its stand. His mother was in her room but he was taking no chances. Going back outside, young Gabriel Polk hid as he dialled the emergency services number, crouching down in the chill October air. When the operator came on the phone, he didn't hesitate before announcing what he was convinced had happened. His mother had killed his father.

Susan Polk was lying in bed when she heard her youngest son make his anguished call. What passed through her mind as she realised the nightmare she'd kept at bay for the past 24 hours was about to become sickeningly real? Had she by that time so rewritten her own truth that the horrible memories had been wiped clean?

When police arrived at the house, instinctively wiping their feet so as not to leave footprints on the polished floors or the expensive-looking rugs, Susan denied knowing where her husband was. Hearing he was dead, she made another of the bizarre statements for which she would later become infamous: 'Oh well, we were getting a divorce anyway.'

Over the following two days, Susan continued to deny any knowledge of what had happened to Felix. She'd had no idea he was dead, she told police – she hadn't heard or spoken to him. When crime scene investigators discovered strands of Susan's hair in Felix's clenched fist she changed her story. She had killed him, she admitted, but it had been self-defence. Her husband – 50 pounds heavier than she was – had cracked when he realised she really was going to leave him and had attacked her with a knife. As a battered wife who'd withstood her husband's violence for years, she'd been only too aware what he was capable of. Killing him had been an instinctive act of self-preservation.

Going against her version of events was the fact that her husband had sustained a total of 27 knife wounds – 5 of them serious – while she herself escaped with reddened eyes, a welt on her shoulder and bite marks to her hands.

Susan Polk's trial in the summer of 2006 was one of the most sensational in recent years. The meek-voiced, reed thin Californian housewife who painted herself as the innocent victim of systematic domestic abuse had publicly fallen out with a succession of attorneys appointed to her defence. Among them most notoriously, was Daniel Horowitz whose own wife had been brutally murdered at the start of Susan's aborted first trial.

By the time the second trial was underway, Susan had decided to do away with legal counsel and represent herself in court. Testifying against her as two key prosecution witnesses were her own sons, Gabriel and Adam.

You'd think that when a mother is up on a murder charge that could put her in prison for life, there might be some sympathy from her own children, some soft words, despite what she is alleged to have done. You'd think that when a son is up on the witness stand, forced to give evidence about an event that has left him traumatised, there might be some gentleness from his mother but that didn't happen here.

When Susan Polk cross-examined her youngest son Gabriel it was the first time she'd spoken to him in three years. For four days she subjected him to a barrage of often bizarre questions, which the judge labelled as 'bordering on the abusive' and aimed at establishing less what had happened on the night of 13 October and more what kind of mother she'd been. But Gabriel never wavered from his conviction about her guilt.

'Isn't it true,' his mother asked him during a dispute over how tall he'd been at the time of a school yard fight, 'that you were not the big guy that you are now?'

'Between the four years when you murdered my Dad and now... yeah, I grew a lot,' was the unbending reply.

From Gabriel's evidence emerged a picture of a family in crisis, propelled on a downward slide into bitterness and violence by a delusional mother.

'I do have good memories,' Gabriel told his mother on the

witness stand. 'I do love you, but there's terrible memories with the good memories.'

Adam Polk – by this time 23 – was even more brutal in his dealings with his mother, calling her 'bonkers' and 'the embodiment of evil'. Typically, Susan had a ready explanation for her sons' condemnation. They'd recently bought a civil wrongful death case against her and settled for $300,000. Their motive for wanting her proved guilty, she asserted, was financial.

Susan's third son Eli, who by the time of the trial was serving time for an unconnected assault on an ex-girlfriend, was the only one of her children to testify in her favour and back up her allegations of domestic abuse. The almost unnatural closeness of the bond between mother and son gave rise to speculation about coaching between the two and even – some commentators suggested – a possible incestuous relationship.

'I miss you so much that it is driving me crazy,' Eli wrote to her while she was in jail awaiting trial. 'I love you enough to burn what I am and meet you in the afterlife.'

The trial not only set brother against brother and mother against son, but also saw Susan herself pitted against practically everyone in the courtroom. Her angry outbursts at officials, from the judge right down to the court reporter, and her constant interruptions and demands for a mistrial brought her 'victim' status into serious question. The prosecutor, who she'd variously labelled a 'moral creep', 'deceitful' and 'disgusting', later declared her the 'most hateful' person he'd ever come up against.

Susan – who accused crime scene investigators of tampering with evidence – brought several witnesses to the stand in her defence. These included a therapist who agreed that she could indeed be psychic and a medical expert who testified that Felix was more likely to have died from a heart attack than from his wounds.

In the end, though, it was not enough to convince a jury. On Friday, 16 June 2006, Susan Polk was found guilty of second-degree murder. The jury didn't find enough evidence to prove she premeditated the murder but was equally not convinced she acted in self-defence. In court to hear the verdict were Adam and Gabriel Polk, who listened impassively as their mother's future was sealed with that one word: 'guilty'.

On 23 February 2007, Susan Polk – who suggested during her trial that Winona Ryder might be a good choice to play her in a movie of her story – was sentenced to life imprisonment with a minimum of 16 years.

Prosecutor Paul Sequeira has no doubt she will serve the full term. 'She has shown no remorse. She is still defiant and I think she will be until she draws her last breath.'

CHAPTER SEVEN

BODY IN THE BOOT

The Hotel Mercure, just outside St Albain, near the French town of Macon, is not the sort of place that sticks in the mind. A modern, 86-room building, it's more acclaimed for its accessible location just off the A6 Autoroute du Soleil than for its ambience. Tourists heading down through the centre of France might break up their journey there before heading on towards more fashionable holiday spots such as Provence or the French Riviera. Otherwise it's mostly used by businessmen taking advantage of its convenient location and conference room facilities or by golfers attracted to the nearby courses. Occasionally guests may stay a few days, perhaps sampling a bit of wine-tasting in the surrounding Burgundy vineyards, exploring Macon or even venturing into nearby Lyons. But mostly it's used as a mid-route stopover where weary drivers can recharge by the outdoor swimming pool, or just take in a meal in the restaurant before they flop into bed for the night, continuing their journey the next day.

When Derek Symmons pulled up into the car park at the Mercure on 6 September 2005, there was nothing to suggest he was anything but a normal tourist on his way down to the South. The BMW he was driving had British number plates, suggesting he'd probably got straight onto the Autoroute after arriving in Calais, and had decided this was as good a place as any to decamp for the night. The 62-year-old electrical engineer looked slightly wide-eyed and haggard as he arrived in the hotel's rather soulless lobby with its circular seating bench and curved reception desk, all in various shades of beige and brown. But then most guests seemed that way when they arrived, after hours spent staring at the tail lights of the car in front on the endless French motorway.

Having checked in, Derek went off to his room but when he reappeared in the bar some time later he showed no signs of being refreshed or rested. Instead he seemed agitated and distressed. Despite his smart, obviously expensive clothes, he had an almost wild look about him. Curious hotel staff would soon discover why. 'I've done something terrible,' he told the hotel's receptionist. 'I've killed my wife. Her body is in the boot of my car.'

★ ★ ★ ★ ★

The private Loudwater estate near Rickmansworth is one of Hertfordshire's most exclusive addresses. With its leafy lanes and river views, all within a mile of the M25, it contains some of the most desirable real estate in the country. The homes on Lower Plantation, Loudwater are among the most sought after in the area. Large detached buildings with landscaped gardens and, in several cases, swimming pools, they are an estate agent's dream and fetch upward of £1 million, sometimes several times that.

When Derek and Christine Symmons bought their modern, six-bedroom home there in the early 1980s, with its decorative shutters on the upper windows, they were really trading up, as well as stretching themselves to their financial limit. Although Derek was forging his way up the career hierarchy, he wasn't yet earning a fortune and Christine didn't bring in much from her job as a part-time hairdresser. But they knew Loudwater would be the perfect place to bring up their two children, Mark and Claire, even if they did have to mortgage themselves up to the hilt to live there.

It was a decision they wouldn't regret. The Loudwater house provided them with a comfortable, stable base in which to raise their family, plus friendly neighbours to share barbecues in the summer and Christmas drinks. Above everything, it was a home rather than just a house and they soon became very settled there, particularly after

Derek's earnings increased and they no longer lived in dread of not being able to make the monthly repayments.

But as their financial position improved, their relationship began to show signs of strain. Derek had always been inclined to be moody and the family came to dread his quick flares of temper and sulky outbursts when things weren't going his way. In addition, his growing reputation as an electrical engineer involved projects that took him away from home for long periods of time. An outwardly ebullient, sociable man, he wasn't the type to sit around in lonely hotel rooms during these extended trips. He loved to go out and engage with new people, especially women.

Derek was never a particularly handsome man, neither did he wear his accumulating years with a huge amount of dignity, choosing to dye his hair reddish-brown rather than confront his greying reflection in the mirror. But he did have great charm and of course the sex appeal that comes with having monetary success. He never seemed to have trouble finding female company while away working.

Christine might have been based at home but she'd been married since 1968 and she knew her husband well enough to guess what he was up to. Not that he bothered to be terribly discreet. She'd once driven past his workplace and seen him kissing another woman outside. Another time she opened a Christmas card from one of his lovers.

With every fresh betrayal, the marriage crumbled slightly further although from the outside it appeared as strong as ever. Friends and neighbours often commented on how great it was to see a couple so happy together after so many years. In private, Christine was losing patience with her moody, wayward husband, however. She'd given him so many chances and he just seemed to throw them all back in her face.

As Derek reached his mid-fifties the situation became even more desperate. He'd always been sensitive about his sexual virility, having suffered a bout of impotence around the time of his mother's death. He'd been unusually – some said unnaturally – close to his mother and her death had hit him very hard. Around 2000, the impotence returned, plunging him into a crisis of confidence and putting further strain on the marriage. Only Viagra enabled him to perform in bed, something that both infuriated and panicked him in equal measures.

The couple began to argue more frequently and more violently. Derek's paranoia about his sexual inadequacy increased and he became convinced Christine was belittling him behind his back. He even bugged the house in the hope of catching her ridiculing him to her friends. But Derek's concerns about his sexual prowess did little to stop his philandering ways. In 2004, he began an affair with Myra Croney, a divorced teacher he'd met through an internet dating site. Christine found out about the affair a year later in the most humiliating of ways when her mobile rang. Having answered, it quickly became clear that the caller had pressed the dial button by accident and she could hear two voices. One was her husband's and the other, she was shortly to discover, belonged to his mistress. Listening in to the conversation, Christine felt as if someone had grabbed hold of her insides and was twisting and squeezing them in a kind of excruciating torture.

'I love you,' the female voice said at one point. Soon after she heard her husband laugh crudely. 'You don't need to wear knickers in the summer,' he told the woman. Hanging up, Christine felt sick. Even though she'd known Derek hadn't been faithful to her over the years, having to listen to him being intimate with another woman was painful beyond belief. How could he use that same loving tone of voice he'd once saved for her on some stranger? And how could he laugh and joke without being torn apart by guilt at what he was doing?

She felt completely destroyed by what she'd inadvertently heard. Yet somehow, she managed to find the self-control to keep the information to herself until she'd had more chance to work out what was going on, and what she was going to do about it. When Derek got home, Christine secretly fished his wallet out of his jacket pocket and started to search through, looking for evidence of what she'd heard on the phone. Once again the nausea welled up inside her as she came across the very clues she'd been seeking – condoms and Viagra.

There can be few more upsetting discoveries than finding out the person you think you know best is practically a stranger with a whole double life you'd never suspected. But Christine was wary of Derek and his unpredictable temper. She knew that confronting him about his affair could unleash a vitriolic backlash and she didn't know if she was strong enough to withstand it. For a few nightmarish weeks, Christine kept her unwelcome knowledge to herself, constantly revisiting it in her mind as you might keep probing a painful ulcer with your tongue.

Then one evening at a wedding reception, Christine cracked. 'I know you're having an affair,' she told her stunned husband. Derek was shocked. He had no idea his wife had even the slightest idea about his latest paramour. He told her he was sorry and he said it wouldn't happen again. What's more, he even emailed his children flamboyantly confessing his misdemeanours and claiming it was the first time he'd strayed.

'I swear on your life I'm telling the truth,' he told his daughter, dramatically.

'Liar,' she replied.

But Christine Symmons had had enough. She was fed up with the rows and the bullying, and with being treated with such blatant disregard. While she might be a grandmother she was still in her fifties (well, just) and she'd kept herself trim and attractive. Her copper-coloured hair always impeccably styled and highlighted, her nails perfectly polished. Why shouldn't she make a new start? Why shouldn't she have the chance of maybe meeting someone else? Her husband seemed to have no trouble doing that.

Although she was afraid of her domineering husband, Christine worked up the courage to consult a solicitor about a possible divorce. The children, of course, were grown up now but she wanted to know exactly where she stood financially and legally. She was also terrified of how Derek would react to her trying to make a life without him. His behaviour had been so erratic recently, so volatile. If she was going to take a stand against him, she wanted to be sure she had the full backing of the law.

Derek was flabbergasted by his wife's new determination. The fact that she'd actually found out her legal rights meant that she really was serious about splitting up. What would happen to the house? What about the His and Hers BMWs and all the exotic holidays? If the marriage broke down, there was so much that he stood to lose. The idea was just unthinkable.

'I want a trial separation,' Christine demanded, determinedly keeping her voice firm so as not to betray the quivers of fear that shot through her as she stood up to her controlling husband. Shocked into uncharacteristic acquiescence Derek agreed to move into the granny annexe in the house. At least it was less final than a divorce. He also agreed to stop his affair and to start marriage counselling.

For a few weeks, the couple lived like relative strangers in their different parts of the house. It was like being in a kind of limbo – not exactly housemates, but not lovers either. Then, halfway through August 2005, Christine discovered that Derek was still seeing Myra Croney. Finding her number in his mobile, she called and confronted the other woman only to be told that Derek was passing himself off as separated following his 'unhappy marriage'.

That was the last straw. Christine was now determined to break up from her cheating husband and start a new life. But she knew he'd never want to give her up and nor the comfortable existence they'd built up together, at least not without a huge struggle. She was torn between feeling elation at the idea of starting over and terror at what Derek might do to her when she finally pulled the plug on their marriage. He was so unpredictable, so threatening, she confided to her friends and her daughter. There really was no telling what he was capable of.

On 5 September, the Symmons had their first session with a marriage guidance counsellor. As expected, it had been a tense encounter and emotions were still running high as they pulled up on their stone-cobbled, hedge-lined driveway that evening. Christine tried to focus on positive things to take her mind off the altercation she was sure was coming. She thought about her gorgeous new grandchild. The following day, as usual, she'd be going round to her daughter Claire's home to help her bath and tend to her baby. She loved the fact that Claire lived near enough for her to be a fully involved grandmother and it was such a marvellous distraction from all the problems at home. All she had to do was get through that night.

But as they let themselves in through the porticoed porch, the tension that had been building in the Symmons' relationship for the past months reached bursting point. A bitter argument broke out between husband and wife. Derek would later claim Christine taunted him with slights about his beloved mother and about his sexual prowess. 'Yeah, well how come I was with Myra just a couple of days ago,' he bragged. 'She certainly had no complaints.' That's when Christine lost control and lunged for his neck, said Derek. The only way he could stop her from strangling him, he claimed, was to grab her neck in return. When she slumped to the ground he realised he'd gone too far.

However, the evidence points to a different version of events. Christine was a slight woman and not given to violence. Furthermore, when Derek was examined after being arrested in France, there was no bruising on his neck. Far more likely is it that Derek was riled up by the counselling session and angered by something his wife had said. In a rage at seeing the writing on the wall spelling out 'divorce', he attacked his wife of 38 years, beating her around the legs and arms, and squeezing her throat with his hands until every last breath of air was gone from her body.

Having realised what he'd done, Derek must have panicked. His first thought would be to get the body out of the house and as far away as possible. Somewhere in the house or the shed he had some plastic sheeting. Glad to have something else to focus on, he went off in search of it. On his return he carefully wrapped up his wife's lifeless body and hoisted it up, staggering outside with it before heaving it into the boot of the larger BMW. Then he went inside to tidy up and change, grabbing his passport and throwing some things into a bag. During the course of his preparations he'd decided what he was going to do: he was going to drive to the south of France.

Put yourself in Derek Symmons' shoes. You've been with your partner for the best part of 40 years. Though you might have cheated on her, bullied her and even perhaps fantasised about how your life would be without her, she's always been a constant. But now you've killed her; you've murdered the mother of your children. In a moment that can never be undone you've destroyed your family, your home, everything you've built up over the years. How do you deal with such knowledge? How do you process such shock?

According to Derek, he simply went into a kind of automatic state where he remembers nothing of the long hours following the murder or of getting back into the car in the early morning and circumnavigating a still-sleeping London on the way to Dover. Nor could he remember the cross-channel ferry journey or driving the car out of the Calais docks and negotiating his way onto the French motorway. His trance came to an abrupt end late in the afternoon, he later claimed, when his mobile rang as he was driving through the French countryside. It was his daughter Claire. Alarmed that her mother hadn't shown up to look after the baby, she was trying to track her down.

Christine had been due at her daughter's house at 6.15 that evening to take over baby-duties for a while. She did this at least five times a week and new mum Claire really depended on those visits. With her doctor husband out of the house most of the day, she found it impossible to get on with anything and look after the baby at the same time – some days it was hard enough even to get dressed. So when her mum hadn't turned up at the usual time, Claire started to worry. With the baby over her shoulder, she'd paced up and down the living room, straining to hear the sound of her mum's car door slamming. It would be the welcome signal that she'd have some respite – a little time to clear up or take a bath, or just sit down for a moment and close her eyes. Increasingly impatient, she'd tried ringing her parents' house but there was no answer. Eventually she decided to call her father's mobile.

'Have you seen Mum?'

That question jolted the 62-year-old out of his traumatised state and into the reality of what he'd done. 'I have done something terrible,' he told his daughter. 'You will never forgive me.' The words formed an icy claw around Claire's heart. Her mum had been so scared of her father recently and it was so unlike her to fail to turn up when she said she would. She couldn't bear to think what it might all mean.

'Why don't you come over and we'll talk about it?' Claire asked, with trepidation.

'I can't, I'm in France,' came the reply.

His daughter just couldn't make sense of it, didn't *want*

to make sense of it. A horrible sickening feeling was gathering inside her.

'Where's Mum?' she asked again.

'She's with me,' Derek replied. 'There was a struggle and she's dead.'

The horror building inside 30-year-old Claire came gushing to the surface in one piercing scream. 'Tell me you're joking,' she begged. '*Please* tell me you're joking.' Above all things she wanted to hear her father's strange voice return to normal and for him to say "Course I am, you silly thing! You didn't think I'd really killed her, did you?' But in her rational brain she knew that wasn't going to happen. In the course of one phone call, her safe and comfortable world had been twisted into a nightmare and nothing would ever be the same again.

A short while later, even as his distraught daughter was on the phone to police in the UK, telling them what had happened, Derek Symmons pulled his BMW estate into the car park of the Hotel Mercure. He had an idea in his head that he'd stay one night and then continue down to the south of France in the morning. He had friends there and he'd see them for the last time then perhaps turn himself in. But the conversation with Claire and a subsequent conversation with her brother, where he'd repeated his story and affirmed Christine's body was in the boot of the car, released the flood of emotions he'd been damming up since the previous evening. This was no game – he really had killed his wife.

Derek couldn't hold it in any more – he had to tell

someone. He was racked with sorrow and remorse for what he'd done, although whether his distress was for his wife or for himself is something that will never be fully known. Wild-eyed and grief-torn, he approached the reception desk.

'I've done something terrible – I've killed my wife,' he said.

★ ★ ★ ★ ★

On 11 December 2006, Derek Symmons was found guilty of murdering his wife and sentenced to life imprisonment with a minimum of 16 years. A jury at St Albans Crown Court took less than 3 hours to dismiss his claims of having killed Christine in self-defence after her taunts about his sexual prowess sparked a violent row.

His children have disowned him. 'Words cannot begin to describe the most dreadful, devastating feeling you get when you are told your mother is dead and has been killed by your father,' a still-grieving Claire said after the court case.

By the time he gets out Derek Symmons will be an old man. He may even die in prison. If his wife had divorced him, the one thing of which he was so afraid, then he would have lost his high standard of living and perhaps his home and maybe even part of his pension.

As it is, he's lost everything.

CHAPTER EIGHT

HORROR IN
THE MIRROR

If you work in Manchester's bustling city centre – a diverse but intense and demanding metropolis, where high commerce butts right up against student culture and gang members rub shoulders with television producers – few places can be more relaxing to come home to at night than Bowdon, near Altrincham.

The genteel, leafy Cheshire suburb, with its wide, tree-lined avenues and well-preserved old stone parish church, offers a perfect contrast to the vibrant multiculturalism of Manchester itself. Nightlife is most likely to be a quiet glass of wine in the Stamford Arms pub or maybe a charity ball. On summer weekends tennis and cricket are staple activities here, as is competitive croquet at the local sports club. In this part of the world, winters can be harsh but the regular church fundraisers and games of bridge in front of roaring log fires take the chill off the outside air.

Little wonder then that Christopher Lumsden, a respected partner in the international law firm Pinsent Masons – which had offices in Manchester, as well as other, key UK cities – always looked forward to returning home to Bowdon and never more so than on Fridays. After a taxing working week he was finally able to take off his pinstriped suit and relax. Of course it didn't hurt that 'home' to the high-flying lawyer was Oakleigh, a £2m, stone-built mansion surrounded by rolling lawns and spreading trees. Or that his wife Alison who'd given up a successful career to devote herself to looking after the house and the couple's two children always made sure there was a warm, welcoming atmosphere in their otherwise imposing home.

On Friday 11 March 2005, 52-year-old Christopher was relieved to find there were no social engagements on – just a cosy evening at home with Alison, or Ali, as she was known to her many friends in the village and at the local tennis club, where she was social secretary. Never quite as sociable as his outgoing wife, Christopher had become more reclusive since being diagnosed with a rare muscle wasting disorder in November of the previous year. The discomfort in his back, which he'd always put down to an old rugby injury, turned out to be a progressive and debilitating illness that would eventually put him in a wheelchair and might even kill him within three years. For the previously fit, tennis-loving lawyer it was a shattering blow, and one which months later he was still having extreme difficulty coming to terms with. It wasn't the prospect of dying that bothered him, more the idea of living with an incurable illness that was only going to get worse.

On one occasion he'd even thought about killing himself, although after driving into the countryside to contemplate suicide, having dropped his wife off at a tennis game, he'd decided to give life another chance. But that evening he was trying not to dwell on depressing thoughts; he just wanted to have a quiet and relaxing time with the wife he'd adored for more than 25 years. As their children – Thomas, 20, and Kate, 17 – were away from home, it would be a chance for the two of them to catch up and perhaps repair a bit of the distance his recent reclusive behaviour had wrought in their marriage.

But tonight Ali seemed on edge. Usually vivacious and gregarious, the blonde 53-year-old with the big smile that seemed to put people from all walks of life at ease despite her cut-glass accent, was unusually reserved and distracted. At dinner, where she'd normally have held forth about what was going on in the village, or what she'd done in London the weekend before, she was uncharacteristically silent. Afterwards, when they'd just settled in to watch television and Christopher was finally beginning to feel the stress of his working week lift from his shoulders, Ali got to her feet. With a decisive movement, she switched off the TV and turned to face her husband.

'I've got something to tell you,' she began.

Christopher blinked at her in surprise, his round, pudgy face registering an expression of bewilderment. What could she possibly have to say that would merit this dramatic fanfare? But what Ali told him that night shook up everything he'd ever taken for granted or held as true: she'd been having an affair for the last month with a family friend and she wanted a divorce. In his professional capacity Christopher had developed the skill of remaining outwardly calm and dispassionate when confronted by shocking or unsettling news, processing it internally so that his response, when it came, would always be measured and thoughtful. This is how he dealt with his wife's revelation that she'd fallen in love with Roger Flint.

The Flints – Roger and his wife Fiona – belonged to the same social set as Alison and Christopher. The four sometimes played doubles together at the tennis club or met for occasional games of bridge. One year the two families even spent part of their holidays together when they'd coincidentally ended up in the same vicinity. Though they weren't close companions, they were definitely friends, so the double betrayal hit Christopher hard – 'I felt stunned and numb. Alison had betrayed me with somebody I regarded as a friend. She abandoned me.'

Rubbing more salt on the wound was the timing of their affair, which had begun on 12 February, just weeks after the funeral of Christopher's mother, whose death had hit her son surprisingly hard.

It's often said that the worst thing for betrayed partners to comprehend is not that their beloved could do such a terrible thing to them, but that it wasn't done 'to them' at all, that they were completely inconsequential in the face of this new and exclusive, all-absorbing passion. When Ali had danced with Roger Flint at a birthday party at Bowdon Lawn Tennis Club, she just wasn't thinking about Christopher – in fact it was a relief to have some time without him. They'd been so remote from one another recently she'd even moved into the spare room, ostensibly to get relief from his snoring, but also to allow them both some space to think. His illness seemed to have taken the spirit out of him, so that, even if he had been physically able, he had no interest in doing all the things they'd previously loved to do together. She was becoming increasingly frustrated.

When Roger, who also had two children, confessed he'd been harbouring feelings for her, it must have seemed like a window opening to let fresh air into what was becoming a rather stifling existence. Just when she'd begun to think nothing exciting would ever happen to her again, when she'd resigned herself to living in an increasingly unsatisfying marriage, here was a man offering her a chance of something new, making her feel attractive and vital again.

The couple started meeting for lunch, talking for hours and making each other roar with laughter. Being together felt so right. They even managed to get away together for a couple of days at the beginning of March. Alison said she was going to London but instead she and Roger stayed in Cornwall. By the time they got back, she knew her marriage was over, but she was dreading breaking the news to Christopher. He'd been through such a lot recently and she knew it might look as though she was abandoning him just when he needed her the most. But she was 53 years old and this kind of opportunity may not come again. This was her chance of happiness and she intended to seize it with both hands.

After dropping the bombshell, Ali broke down in tears from a mixture of guilt and relief. She was glad Christopher, though naturally devastated, seemed to be taking it so stoically and she allowed herself to hope that this might be that rarest of animals, the amicable divorce. At 9.46 that evening, she sent a text to her lover:

'It's done. All calm and reasonable as expected so can't stop crying at moment. He wants to speak 2u b4 u speak to F [Roger's wife, Fiona]. I'm exhausted.'

After the whirlwind of her romance with Roger, followed by the build-up to the confession and the confession itself, Alison felt she'd been through the emotional wringer. Her mind raced with conflicting emotions – excitement about the future, grief for the past, and above all, a kind of hammering awareness that nothing in her life would ever be the same again. An hour after the first text to Roger Flint, she sent another one:

'Darling, we must talk tomorrow AM. I am feeling huge relief but I'm also overwhelmed at the enormity of what I've just done.'

For Alison, telling Christopher she wanted a divorce represented the closure of one chapter of her life and the beginning of another. For her husband, however, it just spelled the end: end of his marriage, end of his happiness, end of his life. He was already facing the loss of his health and now he was going to lose his wife as well. Over the next few days he sank into depression and became obsessed with the thought that Ali was turning her back on him because he was an invalid and could no longer keep up with her. Again and again, he tried to get her to reconsider, offering to move jobs, houses, even towns, if she'd just give their marriage another chance. With every refusal, his spirits plummeted further. At his office, he'd spend hours pondering the financial implications of a divorce and thinking about cutting her out of his will and reducing her share in joint assets. It was one way of trying to get her to pay for what she was doing to him.

As he'd asked his wife not to tell anyone about their separation until the end of the school year so it wouldn't affect their daughter's AS-level exams, Christopher knew he had a little time to try to sort things out. At heart, however, he was well aware this was just delaying the inevitable and that financial retribution wasn't going to change anything. Ultimately he was still going to be left alone to cope with his ever more debilitating illness, while Ali and her strong, fit lover built an new exciting life for themselves. It didn't help that Ali gave him suggestions on how to make things better for himself. 'She said I should get a life and date some people,' Christopher would later tell a court. 'I was like a drowning man needing a life raft.'

Reluctantly Christopher went to see a divorce lawyer, breaking down as he talked through details of the forthcoming separation. The few people he confided in were sympathetic and gave him the speech all soon-to-be-divorced people become very familiar with – you'll meet someone else, you'll enjoy being single, plenty more fish in the sea. So, on Tuesday, 15 March, at a business function at Manchester Art Gallery, Christopher decided to try to implement a more positive approach. After complimenting blonde Debbie Sandler, the PR expert who'd organised the party, he asked whether she accepted invitations to drinks. At first, Debbie was delighted, thinking the lawyer was talking on a professional level about perhaps getting her some business with his firm, but his next words disabused her of that notion: 'I'm going through a divorce. It would be nice to have someone to talk to.'

Debbie had no interest in becoming a shoulder for a

reluctantly single, middle- aged lawyer to cry on so she made her excuses and left. The following morning – Wednesday, 16 March – her phone rang. It was Christopher Lumsden. 'I'm a man of my word,' he told her, with forced jollity. 'I said I'd ask you out for that drink.' Debbie was mortified. She knew she was going to have to be blunt so he didn't get the wrong idea and she told him clearly that she wouldn't be going out with him. 'That's a pity,' Christopher replied, his lawyer's training helping to smooth over any traces of hurt or self-pity. 'You see, I'm going away very soon and I have no idea how long I'll be gone.' Was it a way of saving face having had his advances rebuffed? Or was Christopher Lumsden predicting his own future before it had even begun?

That evening he went to see a colleague of his who'd been through a bitter separation of his own. Like anyone who's gone through a divorce, said to be the second most traumatic life-changing event after bereavement, he needed the reassurance of talking to someone who had been where he was now and come through the other side. Again, the usually tightly buttoned lawyer wept as he talked about what was happening and how completely powerless he felt. First his health and now his marriage were being snatched away from him and there was nothing he could do.

When he got back to Oakleigh, Ali was out. The house seemed dark and cold. Christopher must have wondered if that was how it would be from now on – coming home to an empty house. His mood slipped even further into darkness at the thought of all the lonely nights to come. Miserably, he got ready for bed, putting on his pyjamas and going into the spare room where Ali had been sleeping to turn on the electric blanket so it would be warm for her when she got home. Then he went back to his own bed and started reading.

Ali, meanwhile, had had a lovely evening. She and Roger Flint had enjoyed dinner together at a restaurant in nearby Plumley. They'd both been feeling so much better after confessing their feelings to their respective spouses. Though obviously there had been some deeply unpleasant, upsetting scenes, by and large everyone seemed to be behaving in a remarkably civilised way. Things seemed to be 'moving along without too much upset,' Roger Flint would comment later on. The two lovers were just relieved that everything was now out in the open and soon they'd be able to be together.

After leaving the restaurant, they drove home to Altrincham in separate cars, finally parting at about 10.25pm. That was the last time Roger Flint would see Ali Lumsden alive. What went through Ali's head as she pulled up outside the storybook home in which her marriage had slowly suffocated to death? Did she wonder about Christopher – lying in bed waiting for her to return – and how he'd cope when there was no longer anyone to wait up for? Or was her mind so firmly fixed on the glorious future so nearly within reach that she had no thoughts to spare for what had passed and was now done?

Letting herself in through the heavy door, Ali made her way straight upstairs. Seeing Christopher's light still on, she went into the bedroom and sat down at the dressing table to take off her make up, as she had done so many times before over the course of their marriage. That's when something inside Christopher Lumsden snapped. His own memories of that night are sketchy. Did Alison say something about his deteriorating health? Was the word 'cripple', which he later claimed to have heard spoken out loud, just whispered inside his own mind? Did he get an image of his wife with Roger Flint, together, as they had been only minutes before?

Whatever the trigger, an immense, overpowering wave of anger swept through him as his soon-to-be ex-wife sat at her dressing table with her back to him. Raising himself to his feet, he slid open a bedside drawer and pulled out a 12-cm knife that had been kept there ever since a burglary some years before. Making his way silently around the foot of the bed, he came up behind his wife and there was a brief moment when their eyes met. If Christopher had stopped then, snapping out of whatever terrible frenzy had taken over him, how different would life be now for himself, for his children and for Roger Flint? Instead, a part inside of him broke that night which propelled him onwards. As Ali Lumsden turned from the dressing table mirror and tried to stand, her husband brought the knife down. Again, and again, and again…

★ ★ ★ ★ ★

When the phone rang at 10.40pm on 16 March 2005 in Gawsworth Hall, a beautiful half-timbered Tudor stately home in Macclesfield, Cheshire, the First Lady of the manor, Elizabeth Richards, was surprised to hear her normally composed brother sounding almost incoherent. When she finally managed to understand what Christopher Lumsden was telling her – 'I think I have killed Alison' – her initial confusion turned to horror.

Leaving their son Rupert at home, Elizabeth and her husband Timothy immediately got into the car and drove straight to Bowdon. Navigating the dark country roads, the same thoughts kept going round their heads. Surely this would turn out to be some ghastly mistake. Surely there'd be some reasonable explanation. Pulling up outside the house at 11.10pm, they decided Timothy would stay in the car while his anxious wife went in to confront her brother.

Always an imposing house, Oakleigh was eerily quiet and apart from a glimmer of light in the hallway, in total darkness. Not knowing what to expect, Elizabeth rang the bell. The sound echoed in the unnatural stillness of the March night. Bending down, she opened the flap of the letterbox. 'Christopher,' she called sharply. Finally, the door was opened. In the hallway stood Christopher Lumsden, renowned financial lawyer, his face deathly white, his body shaking. All hope of this being some terrible misunderstanding disappeared as Elizabeth's gaze passed over her brother's pyjamas. They were soaked with blood.

As Christopher slumped onto a chair in the hall, Elizabeth tried to find out what had gone on but her brother, normally so eloquent, was too traumatised to make much sense. 'Is she dead?' she asked him urgently. 'I don't know' was his barely coherent reply. Filled with trepidation, she made her way up the stairs to the main bedroom. At the doorway she hesitated. There are some sights that you know will stay with you forever. For Elizabeth Richards, this would be one of them. Lying in a pool of blood on the floor of the bedroom was her sister-in-law Alison. One glance at her savagely torn neck was enough to convince her that she was dead.

In a state of shock Elizabeth Richards, one of the leading lights in Cheshire's social scene, dialled 999. Then she went out of the house to break the news to her husband, who was still sitting in the car unaware that their family lives had changed forever. 'Alison's dead.' Strange how two words can have such a shattering effect.

Christopher Lumsden was still sitting in the hallway when his sister burst in from the outer porch with her husband. While so much of that night remains a nightmarish blur, Timothy Richards will never forget his first sight of his brother-in-law. 'He was totally motionless, clearly totally traumatised and clearly immensely depressed – it was quite apparent that one should not really speak to him at that point. There was nothing one could say,' he would later remark. Instead, Timothy placed his hand fleetingly on Christopher's head in a gentle gesture of support. There was literally nothing else he could think of to do.

On 10 February 2006, a crumpled, shaken Christopher Lumsden hoisted himself painfully to his feet to hear a jury at Manchester Crown Court clear him of murder but declare him guilty of manslaughter on the grounds of diminished responsibility. Clearly distressed, the once proud lawyer asked to say a few words before sentencing was pronounced in the hope that he could offer a 'crumb of comfort' to friends and family. 'If there is anything I could do to atone for this appalling tragedy or even to reduce by a small amount the anguish, pain and suffering I have caused, I would do it,' he croaked, choking back the tears.

Christopher Lumsden, who has always maintained he has no memory of the moment he actually killed his wife, received a sentence of five years. While his physical release is not far off, the mental torment of what he did to the woman he calls 'my angel' will haunt him for the rest of his life.

Sometimes the cruellest prison is that of our own minds.

CHAPTER NINE

'I'LL FEED YOU
TO THE PIGS'

Tina Baker let out a long, drawn-out sigh and smoothed a lock of unruly curly black hair back from her face. It was 1998 and she'd just talked to yet another friend who'd passed on a message from her husband Martin. 'He really wants you back, Tina,' the friend had told her. 'He says you're the best thing in his life.'

It was all very well him being all lovey-dovey now, Tina reflected angrily. He hadn't been that way when they'd been living together and he was picking at everything she did, trying to control where she went, who she talked to, what she spent. And would someone who thought you were the light of his life lose their temper with you quite so quickly, saying all kinds of horrible things?

But then Tina couldn't help remembering how kind he'd seemed when they'd first met through a lonely hearts ad some years earlier Martin had placed in a magazine. Although he was a decade older than she herself and his weather-beaten face bore the telltale lines of past disappointments, Martin – or Jed, as he was known to most people – had immediately struck her as a genuine person who said what he meant. Though not exactly an oil painting, with his thin, straggly hair and watery blue eyes, once they got to know each other better and the two discovered a mutual passion for animals, Tina's feelings had gradually deepened into love.

They'd married in May 1996 and at first their joint vision of running a farm and keeping livestock had been enough to keep them together. The day they signed the contract on a 14-acre, £52,000 plot of land that they transformed into Brookfield Farm, in Pennypot Lane, Chobham, Surrey, had been one of the happiest of their lives. Though Martin worked as a machinist at a local engineering company, he'd always wanted to raise livestock, particularly pigs, and Tina just loved any animals, no matter what kind, so building their own farm was the realisation of a dream for both of them.

But, as any relationships expert will tell you, one shared goal isn't enough to keep together a couple with little else in common. Quite soon after they'd walked down the aisle Tina had started to question her wisdom in marrying

Martin. He'd been married before and she worried that the bitterness with which he and his ex-wife had parted didn't bode well for the future of their own relationship. She soon found the 10-year age gap more of a problem than she'd first thought it to be, too. In her mid-thirties when they married, she was still a relatively young woman and determined to get the most out of life, but Martin seemed much more set in his ways. She'd become increasingly unhappy in her marriage and had eventually walked out on her husband in 1998, leaving him in the Egham home they'd shared near to their beloved farm.

But then Martin had started his campaign to try to win her back, calling her friends and family and asking them to pass on messages telling her how much he missed her. He even got his own friends involved to plead on his behalf. Tina slowly found herself softening. Perhaps she'd been too hasty in leaving Martin. He obviously did really love her or he wouldn't be doing so much to win her back. She decided to give the marriage one more chance. It was to prove a very costly mistake.

Together again, the relationship soon settled back into the old, destructive patterns. Tina, naturally a more extrovert, sociable person than her husband, felt stifled by a marriage that felt stale and almost elderly. Coming up to 40, she'd started doing the same as most people confronted by a milestone birthday: taking stock of where she was and asking herself whether this was where she wanted to be. Projecting forwards ten years, did she really want to be approaching 50 and still in this floundering, unsatisfying relationship?

But she was determined to stick it out, not wanting to give up on either Martin or the animals they shared. The doubts refused to go away, however. Then, in May 2002, when Tina was 41, she went out to a school reunion, where she met Derek Poplett. Derek had been an old friend of hers from school. He was her own age, he was part of her history and he made her laugh. Being with Derek made Tina realise all the things she'd been missing out on during her marriage to Martin.

At home things went from bad to worse. Almost as if he could sense her pulling away from him, Martin became ever more controlling. 'What have you done with that money you withdrew from the bank?' he'd demand, holding her accountable for every last penny. They argued more often and said things they both regretted. Increasingly Tina became convinced she couldn't stay in her marriage. 'We never have fun any more,' she tried to explain to her husband. 'I feel like life is passing me by.'

Now past the 40 watershed, Tina felt she didn't have time to sit around, hoping against hope that her relationship with Martin would miraculously improve. In Derek Poplett she'd stumbled across an opportunity for a second chance of happiness. How could she live with herself if she didn't grasp it? But then again Martin was her husband and no matter how much they fought, she still felt guilty about deserting him plus she worried what would happen to the farm she'd worked towards all her life if the two of them should split.

In every failing relationship there exists a twilight zone, an agonising period of limbo, where the person who wants to leave has already moved out in their mind, but remains bodily in the marital home. There, but not quite present, they inhabit their old life like a still-living ghost. While Tina tried to summon up the courage to finally walk out on her marriage, her relationship with Martin became increasingly strained.

On 17 June 2002 everything came to a head. It started when Tina and Martin discovered that four out of their most recent litter of puppies had died. 'That's your fault,' Martin accused her. 'You've been feeding them duck eggs and you've given them salmonella.' For Tina, who'd adored the cute little pups with their barely open eyes and fluffy cotton-wool fur, his remarks were doubly cruel. Not only was she grieving for the loss of the animals but now she also carried the guilt of knowing she might have contributed to their death. 'I don't see how you can be so sure of that,' she argued, gazing at the lifeless little furry bodies with tear-filled eyes. 'We don't know exactly what killed them, nobody does.' But Martin refused to back down.

Tina realised then she'd had enough. If she stayed with Martin she'd always be left feeling like it was her fault when things went wrong. She wanted a relationship built on mutual comfort and support and she no longer believed Martin was capable of giving it to her. That evening she packed her things and left the Egham house to move in with her parents in nearby Shepperton. This time she would never return.

As before when she'd left, Martin Baker was unable to accept his wife walking out on him. She had to come back, he told people. He loved her, they had a life together, a business. As a man who very much needed to feel in control he found it almost impossible to reconcile himself to the fact that Tina had gone and there wasn't a damn thing he could do about it. Even tending the animals and particularly feeding his pigs, which usually gave him a feeling of wellbeing, failed to calm his turbulent emotions. Once again he left repeated messages on her mobile and bombarded friends with calls asking whether they'd seen her or begging them to intervene on his behalf.

When he discovered Tina was seeing Derek Poplett at weekends, Martin's feelings turned from hurt and denial to pure rage. It wasn't just the thought of his wife with another man that so infuriated him, although the very idea of it turned his stomach, it was also the very real possibility that he might lose his farm. If he and Tina divorced, he might end up having to sell the land and the livestock. Even worse was the idea that somehow he'd have to hand it over to Tina and her new boyfriend, and everything for which he'd worked so hard would just fall into the lap of that conniving usurper.

'What does she see in that loser?' he'd rail at his friends. 'He's nothing but a long-haired misfit!' The more he thought about it, the angrier he became. The only thing he could do would be to find Tina and make her sign an agreement to give up her claim to the farm and have her name taken off the deeds.

On 6 July he tracked Tina down to Derek Poplett's home in Sunbury-on-Thames, where he confronted his estranged wife and her reviled new lover. But if he hoped intimidation tactics would persuade Tina to sign away her rights to the farm, he was wrong. She loved that land and the animals. Besides, half of it all was rightfully hers. 'I'm sorry, Jed. I want a divorce,' she told him. 'And I'm not giving up my land.'

Martin Baker fumed. How could it be right that a man could work hard all his life and be faced, at the age of 51, with the prospect of losing it all? Why were women so fickle, so deceitful and so manipulative? His first wife, Gillian, had been the same, he reflected angrily. Never giving him the respect he deserved, always doing things to make him angry. It seemed incredible to him now that he'd let himself be duped again. When Tina had agreed to marry him he'd been the happiest man in the world and now, just six years on, he was facing a second acrimonious and costly divorce.

The more he thought about it the more unfair it seemed to him. He couldn't sleep because of the images that crowded his brain of Tina and her lover living it up on the proceeds of his labour, or, worse still, somehow taking the farm from him and running it themselves. The thought of the pair of them looking after his animals burned across his mind like acid. He had to stop it.

On Monday, 8 July 2002, Tina got ready as usual to go to the farm to feed the animals. As Martin worked at the engineering firm during the day, she generally did the daytime shift and he looked after the early mornings and evenings. She was seen leaving Derek Poplett's house in Sunbury – a fit, active woman with dark, curly hair and a new sparkle in her eye that came from knowing that it was the start of summer and she was loved, and that life was full of new possibilities. Later that day she was due to meet Derek and was then expected for dinner at her parents' in Shepperton. For 41-year-old Tina things were falling into place and she was so relieved she'd taken the chance of starting afresh. Closing the door behind her, she set off out into a world that seemed alive with potential.

That was the last reported sighting of Tina Baker.

Later that same day Fiona Cooper went to tend to her horse in a field near to the Bakers' farm in Pennypot Lane. It was a typical English summer's day with the wild blackberry bushes that lined the potholed path buzzing with bees and muted sunshine filtering through the leaves of the taller trees. Lulled into a sense of calm by the languid summer air, Fiona was surprised to come across Martin Baker at his farm and to notice how nervy and jittery he seemed. Never particularly at ease in company, he appeared particularly agitated and she formed the distinct impression that he couldn't wait to get rid of her.

'Some people are coming over any minute to buy some pigs,' he told her impatiently. Suit yourself, she thought, as she walked off, determined not to let the incident spoil her day. It was only afterwards that something happened to make her think more carefully about Martin's strange behaviour and remember how he'd seemed to be ushering her away. Fiona learned that Tina Baker had quite simply disappeared on that very Monday when she'd been enjoying the peace of the countryside and the silky feel of the horse's gleaming fur under her hand.

She didn't turn up to meet new boyfriend Derek Poplett, nor did she join her parents for dinner. She never returned to pick up her bankcards or her passport, or to be reunited with her faithful Alsatian Samson from whom she was virtually inseparable. There was no sign of her red Vauxhall Astra with the licence plate G392 VVX.

Tina had just vanished.

Questioned about his estranged wife's disappearance, at first Martin Baker told police she must have run off. She'd done it before, he said, disappearing for a couple of weeks without saying where she was and he'd had to trace her by calling all the numbers on her mobile phone bill. She'd obviously decided to pull the same trick again. But when Tina failed to access her bank account or come back for her dog, it became increasingly clear that this was not some impulse getaway. Something sinister had happened to her and police were increasingly sure that Martin knew something about it.

Despite having pestered Tina since she walked out in him the previous month, Martin suddenly quit all attempts to get in touch with her from 8 July onwards. If he really thought she'd done a bunk, wouldn't he have tried to find her? It didn't make sense. Typically, he who liked to keep his business to himself and hated to feel that he was losing control of any situation naturally didn't take kindly to being questioned by the police. 'You'll be digging up my patio next!' he snapped.

Pale from sleepless nights and their faces etched with worry, Tina's parents Geoff and Jean Doyle made endless enquiries and appeals for news of their daughter. It was so unlike her to put them through any needless emotional trauma. They just knew something terrible had happened. Martin, meanwhile, continued to protest that he knew nothing about Tina's whereabouts or what could have befallen her. However, a series of events would soon cast serious doubts on his professions of innocence.

First he had denied being at the farm on 8 July except for an early morning visit to feed the animals. He'd been at work as usual, he told police. And yet Fiona Cooper had seen him there and, according to the engineering company for whom he worked, he'd broken the machine he was working on that day and had been sent home early. Did Tina Baker make it as far as the farm to find her estranged husband already there?

Phone records showed a series of calls made on 8 July from the phone Martin Baker habitually used. One from the vicinity of the farm and one much later at night to Herbie, a friend of his who ran a scrap metal business – Station Breakers in Hayes. Baker denied he'd even had the phone or made the calls. 'I left the phone at the farm,' he claimed. 'Tina must have made the calls.' Things were not looking good for Martin Baker but despite thorough searches, there was no body and no evidence of any crime being committed. As the weeks went on, police despaired of ever getting close to the truth about what had happened to Tina.

The case was featured on the BBC's *Crimewatch* programme. Surrey Police offered a reward of £10,000 for information leading to the arrest and conviction of anyone involved in Tina's abduction or murder. But still there were no leads. But then the police decided to interview Martin's ex-wife Gillian Hopkins. What she told them would throw stomach-turning new light on what was looking like an unsolved mystery. Gillian painted a miserable picture of a violently unhappy marriage. Martin had threatened her at various times throughout their relationship, she said. 'One time he even held a knife up to my throat,' she shuddered.

This was useful background evidence to show what kind

of man Martin really was and what he was capable of, but it was Gillian's next comment that really made officers sit up and take notice. The couple had been arguing about something, as they often did, she explained. When Gillian looked up, something in her husband's expression sent a chill of fear right through her. 'Do you realise I have the power to make you disappear permanently?' he'd hissed at her, his face contorted with barely suppressed rage. 'No one would ever find you. I would cut you up and feed you to the pigs.'

Pigs are known to eat anything. If they're hungry enough, it's reckoned, they'll even eat human flesh. Could Martin have lain in wait for his estranged wife at the farm, killed her and fed her remains to his animals? The thought was at once unthinkably gruesome and horribly plausible. It would explain the lack of bodily evidence and the absence of clues.

In October 2005, more than three years after Tina Baker's disappearance, her husband Martin was arrested and charged with her murder. Police were only too aware that with no body found, despite searches done on the pigswill and manure in the farm, a murder charge would be very hard to prove.

The case came to trial in November 2006. Martin still protested his innocence but the case against him was compelling. In addition to the other evidence, he'd also contacted the local authority to get the council charge on the farm reduced just nine days after Tina disappeared, describing himself as a sole owner. Plus, in April 2003 he'd used his wife's maiden name – Tina Doyle – to get a DVLA licence for a stolen BMW. Neither action pointed to a man that believed his wife was still alive.

On 13 November 2006 Martin Baker was found guilty of murdering his wife. He was sentenced to life imprisonment with a minimum term of 14 years. Tina's body has never been found.

CHAPTER TEN

'OUR KIDS WILL BE ORPHANS'

When Julia Pemberton at first caught sight of the papers laid out on the desk in the study of her five-bedroom home she didn't really register what they were. It was probably something to do with her husband Alan's business, or maybe one of the children had left some schoolwork behind there. But, as she realised what those papers actually represented, idle curiosity turned to puzzlement and then gradually, as the meaning sank in, to horror.

On the desk were copies of her and Alan's wills, plus instructions to the children, William and Laura, of what to do in the event of their parents' deaths. All of a sudden the words Alan had spat at her, his eyes narrow with hatred, started to reverberate around her head.

'I'm going to kill you and then myself. Laura and Will are going to be f★★★★★g orphans and it's your fault!'

At that moment 46-year-old Julia knew beyond a shadow of a doubt that her husband of 22 years was going to murder her. The only question was when – and how.

★ ★ ★ ★ ★

Slanting Hill, near Hermitage, Berkshire, is not the type of place where people live in fear for their lives. Sure, there's crime but with huge detached, multi-million pound properties, surrounded by trees and greenery, it tends to be robbery-related. Burglar alarms and Neighbourhood Watch notices are as much a feature of the houses here as the conservatories and pillared porches.

It's the kind of neighbourhood most of us imagine buying into if we ever win the Lottery. Flashy sports cars nestle next to top-of-the-range 4x4s in the driveways, while the houses are set well back from the unmade road thus ensuring maximum privacy. Despite this, it's still a residential area where neighbours know each other's names and wave as they set off in the mornings for the station or the school run.

When Julia and Alan Pemberton built their dream home here in the late 1990s, they appeared to be the family that had it all. The red brick house, with its porticoed windows and wooden fences, was the embodiment of everything for which they'd worked so hard over the years. Alan now ran a successful financial advice company in Newbury but it had been a hard slog getting to the top of his profession and he'd had to put in long hours before finally reaping the rewards of success. Julia too had earned her good fortune by juggling bringing up her two high-achieving children with her job as a health visitor that often exacted a high emotional toll on her caring, sensitive nature.

Though both were well into their forties, the Pembertons looked a lot younger than their years and had hardly changed in fact from when they'd first met as students at Southampton University. Julia retained her trademark long dark hair, which fell halfway down her back, framing her intelligent, aquiline face. While Alan, with his dark brown hair and unlined complexion, exuded the virile physical energy of a man still in his prime. 'A lovely, lovely couple,' was how a neighbour from Castle Eaton, where they lived in the early years of their marriage, described the Pembertons. 'You couldn't have known a nicer couple.'

The two children completed the textbook family picture. Laura, a strong-willed redhead, was a natural academic high-flyer, excelling at everything she turned her hand to. Her younger brother Will was more of an all-rounder, gifted at music and sport but equally at home on the stage or the football pitch.

As so often happens, things inside the £975,000 dream

house – quirkily named Old Hallowes – were not quite what they seemed to the outside world. Take a glimpse, for a moment, through the wood-framed windows to the living room, dominated by a huge brick fireplace, where the sofas matched the wine-coloured walls and heavy, dark-patterned curtains drape the windows. It should have been the centre of a warm family home yet something was slightly wrong. Some small, but vital part of the picture was missing and, as a result, nothing else quite gelled together, it seemed.

The Pembertons had enjoyed good times together since their 1980 wedding at Holy Rood Church in Swindon, but by the time they moved into their lovingly designed Hermitage home nearly two decades later, the marriage was showing signs of strain. Alan had always had a strong controlling streak. He liked to dominate and to be in charge – that was half the secret of his business success – but increasingly he was showing that side of his nature at home, and particularly to his wife. Though never physically abusive, he went out of his way to show Julia who was boss in their household, periodically subjecting her to vicious verbal attacks. He'd also use money as a means of control, sometimes denying her the means to buy petrol for her car, or even food. Despite being a strong woman, who survived breast cancer, Julia became increasingly intimidated by her husband. She felt she had to be on her guard 24/7 in case she said or did anything to antagonise him. Later, she would later maintain that her husband had also sexually abused her over the years, turning their bedroom into a place to demonstrate power rather than love.

Eventually Julia decided she couldn't carry on living the way they were any longer. She was an intelligent, attractive woman, why should she share her life with somebody who seemed to want a subordinate rather than an equal? It was on 3 September 2002 that she finally worked up the courage to voice the words she'd been thinking about for months: 'I want a divorce.' It's a measure of Alan's iron-fisted self-control that he didn't react straightaway. Instead, he waited a week and then issued her an ultimatum as calmly as if he was negotiating a deal with a client – 'If you don't live with me as my wife, I'll kill you. Then I'll kill myself.' That, he explained, would make orphans of their children. To emphasise the point, he left the wills and letters of instruction out in the study.

Julia was distraught. She knew her husband well enough to know he didn't make idle threats. The following morning she called her brother Frank Mullane, begging for help. In response to the raw desperation in his sister's voice Frank arrived at Slanting Hill as quickly as he could. Clearly traumatised, Julia wanted to report the death threat to the police, but didn't want to drag the children to the police station with her, or to leave them alone in the house. Instead they phoned the police station and were told someone would attend. They waited all weekend in a state of frozen dread but no one arrived.

In the end Julia and Frank went to Newbury Police Station in person, where they spoke at length to the Domestic Violence Co-ordinator, who was convinced by Julia's obvious terror that the setting out of the wills was certainly not some kind of sick practical joke. 'In all my experience ... I have not come across such a cruel act,' the Co-ordinator wrote in a letter of support for Julia. She was advised to seek a Civil Injunction against her husband, barring him from coming near her or the house. In addition, she was assured that her address would be flagged up on the police system so that if she ever made a 999 call, even a silent one, the police would immediately know where to respond and would be on the doorstep within 10 minutes. Julia Pemberton had no clue how dearly this assurance would ultimately cost her.

When the Injunction was served on Alan a few days later, he was predictably enraged but powerless to do anything apart from collect his belongings and leave the house. As she watched him drive his gleaming Mercedes away from Old Hallowes, Julia had a sick, churning feeling in her stomach. Though he'd gone for now, she knew her husband would never, ever leave her alone. And she was right. Over the following weeks, Alan Pemberton kept up a campaign of phone threats against his terrified wife. Julia logged them in a diary. 'It's appalling!' he railed at her in one call. 'I'm destroyed, I'm going to do something not very nice!' In another he told her: 'I've got to have you, I will not tolerate this!' The level of threat increased: 'I will take my revenge. It will devastate Laura and Will. I will not tolerate this!'

Clearly Alan was letting his bitterness turn into a dangerous obsession. In his crazed mind, Julia was no longer a person independent in her own right but an adjunct to him. He wasn't just married to her, he *owned* her, and just as surely as he owned the house they'd spent so long dreaming of, and designed to suit their exact specifications. She'd soon see that she couldn't just erase him from her life, from *their* life. He wasn't about to roll over like an obedient puppy on her command – she'd see who was in charge here. She'd realise that he simply, in his own chilling words, would 'not tolerate this'.

Back in the family home Julia was slowly trying to reclaim back her life after years in the shadow of her controlling husband. When you've been accustomed to living on eggshells, never quite sure from one minute to the next whether something you've done or said is going to antagonise your partner, it can be difficult to adjust to being free. Not that Julia ever really stopped looking over her shoulder – she knew Alan wouldn't forgive or forget – but slowly she started to enjoy the little pleasures of single parenthood. For the first time she could come and go without having to account for where she'd been. She could skip dinner if she felt like it, or hire a romantic movie from the video store.

It felt as if she and the children had been staggering through their lives under an enormous weight that had suddenly been lifted. It would take a while before they walked completely tall again, but at least now they were gradually unfurling, flexing muscles that had all but withered through under-use.

While time was beginning to open up Julia's eyes to a world of potential, it was doing nothing to lessen her husband's obsession. In April 2003, Julia and Will returned, tired but content, from a weekend away. Getting out her keys to open the front door, Julia realised something was very wrong. The key just wouldn't go in the lock. Tentatively she ran a finger over the hard blobs surrounding the keyhole: Super Glue. With a rising feeling of panic, she and Will ran to the back door to see if they could get in that way but again the lock bore the same tell-tale blobs. Julia fought back a wave of nausea as she realised what this meant. Alan, who was supposed to be keeping right away from her and her home, had been to the house.

She called Frank, who immediately got onto the police. Yes, Alan would be interviewed, they were assured. But a follow up call revealed that nothing happened. Similarly, no one came to investigate the locks or to dust for fingerprints. No one seemed to be taking the incident very seriously, except Julia and her family. They were all too aware this was no petulant childish gesture but part of a systematic campaign of revenge – and it was not going to stop there.

The following month there was another chilling reminder that Alan had no intention of giving up and quietly going away. A single letter plopped gently onto the doormat of Old Hallowes. It wasn't the usual post time so it must have been hand delivered. The letter was addressed to Will. Inside was a copy of the Affidavit Julia had sworn when she filed for her injunction. All around the edges were angry, hand-written scrawls. They were death threats, all aimed at Julia.

Surely now the police would have to take them seriously? Who else could have posted the letter apart from Alan, who once again was not supposed to be anywhere near the property? And surely making death threats was considered a crime in itself? Julia was terrified, but at the same time she was also slightly relieved. At least now she had concrete proof that her life was in danger; at least now they'd believe her and something would be done to stop Alan.

Clutching the defaced Affidavit, Frank and Julia once again presented themselves at the police station, where again they had to go through the whole history of the threats and the superglued locks and the injunction. 'This document is vitally important,' Frank entreated the police officer, reluctantly handing over the Affidavit, with its clear and undeniable message of hate and aggression. Walking out of the police station, Frank and Julia were convinced that finally some action would be taken, yet later on when Frank phoned the police station, he was astounded to hear that once again the threats were being brushed under the carpet.

Unbelievably, it would later transpire that the incriminating document had somehow ended up tucked into the police file about the glued locks and the police had no record of it. Yet again, Julia Pemberton felt she was being left to fend for herself, a sitting target for her increasingly enraged husband. Can you imagine how it feels to live in a beautiful home you can't enjoy because it no longer feels safe? Or how you might jump every time the phone rang or freeze to the spot at the sound of a car door slamming outside? To the outside world Julia was a beautiful woman inhabiting a fairytale house. But to those who knew, she was a prisoner, trapped in a web being stealthily spun by her estranged husband – and just waiting for the fate she knew was coming.

In June 2003, an increasingly frantic Julia again met with the Domestic Violence Co-ordinator and had a panic alarm installed in her home. It should have made her feel safe, but it didn't. She was still convinced the police were not taking her situation seriously. 'When my son's bike was stolen, two police officers turned up at my door,' she told a friend. 'When my husband wanted to kill me, nobody wanted to know.'

The police didn't give Julia advice on what to do if Alan followed through with his threats and attacked her. They didn't inspect the house or point out the best escape routes, should she be confronted in her own home. True, the suggestion of moving to a 'safe house' had been mooted, but Julia's strong maternal instincts were to try to retain as much stability as possible for her children. They'd already undergone so much upheaval and emotional trauma that she didn't want them to lose their home as well.

The initial Injunction Julia had against Alan stipulated that if he didn't stay away from her or the house he would be arrested. When that expired in 2003, she had to face the ordeal of another court hearing. Worn down by events and frustrated at what appeared to be indifference on the part of the authorities, Julia was persuaded to allow the Injunction to be downgraded so that a breach would no longer qualify for automatic arrest. Consider the facts: Julia knew her husband wanted to kill her; she knew he'd visited the house on at least two previous occasions despite there being an Injunction against him. Not only this but she also knew the police hadn't pulled him in for questioning. Could you blame her for losing faith in the system supposed to be protecting her? Or imagine how she might agree to take the path of lesser resistance, hoping perhaps that it might dampen the raging fires of Alan's bitterness and anger?

What the authorities didn't know – and Julia tried to block out – was that Alan's rage was already out of control. At the time of the Injunction hearing, it would later transpire that he had already visited websites giving specific instructions on how to carry out a murder. By the autumn of 2003, Julia's nerves were totally frayed. All she thought about, dreamed about, was getting a fresh start away from the house, away from all ties with Alan. She had been momentarily relieved when she'd found out that Alan had a new girlfriend, a woman named Penny Cook, with whom he was living in Bromsash, Ross-on-Wye. 'At least now he'll leave you alone,' friends told her.

But Julia knew Alan's obsession wouldn't allow that to happen. It might have bought her a little time while he readjusted to his new circumstances, but ultimately it wouldn't save her. Alan had vowed to come for her, and she knew he would carry his threat through. It was just a question of whether she could stop him.

When Old Hallowes, the house the Pembertons had built to grow old in, was put on the market by order of the Divorce Court, Julia was filled with conflicting emotions. On the one hand the house had been her children's home and the investment of so many of her and Alan's dreams. But on the other hand, its very air was choked with unpleasant memories, its rooms rank with the smell of fear. Selling the house meant a new start for her, a new home whose rooms didn't bear Alan's imprint, where he couldn't lay claim to the bricks, the mortar, even the inhabitants themselves. By this stage Laura had just started her first term at Cambridge University so it was just Julia and Will left. The Slanting Hill house had been given an impressive £975,000 price tag. Whatever deal was struck, Julia would have enough for a place of her own in which to start over again.

On the other hand, 48-year-old Alan was furious when he learned the house was on the market. The fact that it was the Divorce Court that had instituted the sale rather than his estranged wife made no difference to his warped thinking. In his head this was yet another instance of Julia wresting control from him. It was his house, yet it was being sold without his permission. The whole situation was intolerable, and in the stone-and-timber barn conversion he now shared with new love Penny Cook, Alan Pemberton started to plot his revenge.

When Penny first met the financier, she'd thought him 'the nicest person' she had ever met, witty, intelligent and caring, but now certain things about him started to make her feel slightly uncomfortable. She understood how a person could feel bitter if they'd been kicked out of the house they'd lovingly built without even a possibility of a second chance, as Alan said had happened to him. But recently he seemed unable to think of little else. He was also depressed by the threat of a £361,000 lawsuit from a ex-employee, but it was his estranged wife who was constantly at the forefront of his thoughts. Penny wished he'd just focus on something different – she was sure they could have a great future together if he'd just let go a little bit of the past. But letting go had never been one of Alan's strong points.

Tuesday, 18 November 2003 didn't have the makings of a particularly memorable day. In Hermitage, Will and Julia went about the normal routine they'd fallen into since it had been just the two of them in the house. Even though the undercurrent of menace created by Alan's threats was never far from the surface of their lives, they'd become expert at shutting it off so it didn't interfere with the essential business of school and work.

Over in Ross-on-Wye, however, events were not entirely following the usual pattern. That morning Penny Cook, a legal practice manager, had left for work as usual, leaving Alan behind in bed. When he got up, Alan was restless. Unusually for him, he didn't seem able to concentrate on work. Instead, he just gazed out the window without really seeing the beautiful view of the lake and the acres of garden. Then he reread the article in the local paper that he'd already looked at so many times before. It was a report on a West Berkshire man who'd carried out a triple shooting, killing his girlfriend, daughter and finally himself. What would it feel like, Alan wondered, to see that ultimate fear in another person's eyes and then pull the trigger?

Putting the paper down, he made his way to the locked cabinet which still contained the hunting guns once owned by Penny's ex-husband. Using the key he'd taken earlier, Alan unlocked the little door and reached inside to pull out a 12-gauge shotgun used for clay pigeon shooting. He'd done a fair bit of shooting himself, but all the same it took him a few seconds to adjust to the weight of the gun, the sheer solid bulk of it. A short while later, he sat down with paper and pen to write a note. But this was no casual reminder to a lover, no scribbled explanation of where he was going or when he'd be back.

Did the words come easily to Alan, or did he stare off into space, chewing the end of the pen as he tried to articulate the thoughts whirring round inside his brain? No one will ever know. When Penny finally came across the letter and read Alan's words, it was all too late. 'By the time you read this I will have undertaken a callous act, for which I know I will be severely berated,' he had written. 'No one quite knows the grief and shock I have suffered as a result of the action of my darling wife. My need for revenge is overpowering. As I discussed, I have become obsessed.'

At some point that Tuesday afternoon, he slung the shotgun into the boot of his Mercedes and set off for his £1,000-a-year golf club. Golf always seemed to relax him. There was something about being outside amid the rolling, immaculately kept lawns with nothing to think about but the course of the little white ball, that appealed to his sense of order and control. Plus it really helped focus his mind.

At the club that day other players later reported him being in a 'happy, jokey' mood as he made his way round the course. He didn't seem unduly preoccupied or intense and certainly not like a man with murder on his mind. It just goes to show how deceptive appearances can be.

Alan left the golf club at around 6.30pm. He was due to pick up his son Will for a driving lesson half an hour later, so he just had time to slip into a nearby pub for a quick pint of cider. Other drinkers might easily have supposed that the well dressed, outwardly calm man at the bar that night was a well-to-do businessman on his way home after a casual meeting or indeed a game of golf. They could never have suspected that here was someone who knew he was quite possibly having the very last drink of his life.

Since Alan was legally prohibited from going near his house, he'd got into the habit of picking Will up from further along the road. But this time he turned up at the house itself. Julia and Will froze as the first bangs resounded from the timber framed front door. They didn't need to hear the words he was yelling to know that Alan was in an ugly mood. Will – by now 17 – had no doubt his mother was his dad's intended target. But, as long as he could keep the two apart, he reasoned, then Julia would be safe.

With adrenaline and fear simultaneously pumping round his system, Will Pemberton stepped outside the front door and positioned himself in front of it, blocking his father's path. With any luck he could reason with him, perhaps persuade him to get in the car for his lesson and get them both well away from the house and his mother. If he had read what Alan had written in the note left behind at Penny Cook's Ross-on-Wye home, he would not have felt so confident. 'I hope William does nothing stupid,' it said.

But Alan was now beyond reason. He had waited over a year for his revenge, imagining over and over how it would feel to see Julia cowering in front of him, finally realising the enormity of what she'd done to him. Everything was in order. He wasn't going to let anything or anyone get in the way of him and his intended quarry. Levelling the shotgun, he fired two shots into his son's chest at point blank range. Will, a slight adolescent on the cusp of manhood, slumped to the ground in a blaze of pain and shock.

Alan, however, had already set off round the side of the house without stopping to find out how badly his son was hurt. By now just one thing was on his mind: killing Julia. Through his pain, Will saw his father disappear round the side of the house. He knew he was going to hunt down his mother and he knew he had to try to stop him. Staggering to his feet, he followed after him. 'Stop!' he cried out.

Though once a loving father, proud of his gifted children's achievements, Alan Pemberton turned round and pumped three more shots into his son's chest, stomach and arm. Will fell dead to the ground. How pure a hatred must be to cause a person to kill the very ones they love most just because they stand in their way. And how strong must be the desire for revenge if it overturns the deep-rooted parental urge to protect your young. But when Alan began shooting his way into the house, he was no longer a father, no longer a husband. He was a killer now, and nothing was going to stop him.

Poor terrified Julia had grabbed the phone to dial 999 as soon as she'd heard the first bangs on the door at 7.11pm. While Will had gone outside to remonstrate with his father, she'd begun explaining to the operator what was happening. Remember she'd previously been assured that her address had been flagged up at the police station and that officers would be on the scene within 10 minutes of her making an emergency call? She must have been hoping against hope that Will could keep his father contained for the few minutes until the police arrived. But that hope disappeared with the first blast from the shotgun. 'Oh Jesus Christ, he has hurt my son!' she screamed to the operator near the beginning of what would be a harrowing, 16-minute call. Then: 'Please come quickly, he has let off shots and fired through the window.'

In the meantime, desperate with fear and worry about her son, she hid in the downstairs storeroom, hoping it might afford her some protection. Still the police didn't arrive. More shots were fired. 'He's killed my son!' The cry tore from Julia like a piece of her heart being ripped out. 'Oh my God!' Crouching in the storeroom, unable to lock the door from the inside, she knew her own fate was sealed. If Alan had killed Will, he was not going to let anything stop him getting her too.

'We've got people coming up,' the operator told her in a futile attempt to reassure the terrified woman. But Julia knew nothing was going to save her. 'He's coming through the door – oh God, I've got about one minute before I die!' Loud bangs were heard in the background as Alan Pemberton approached the cupboard where his wife cowered in fear, the phone still in her hand. 'He's coming now!' Julia gasped. Alan burst through the door, his rage by now a hot, white light leading him on to what he had to do. 'You f★★★★★g whore!' he yelled at his sobbing wife. Then he raised his shotgun and fired four times.

After Julia was dead, a heavy silence fell over the house. Alan, his ears still ringing from the blasts and from the sound of blood hammering in his ears, made his way to the stairway. Who knows what went through his mind as he sat down and prepared for the last, inevitable act in his carefully crafted plan. Did he spare a moment of regret for the son, teetering on the brink of adulthood, who'd died so bravely protecting his mother? And did he wonder how a marriage started out with such hope could have gone so horribly, tragically wrong, or how the woman he'd sworn to love forever could now be lying dead in a pool of blood? Of course no one can ever be sure. The only thing we know for certain is that, after killing his son and wife, Alan Pemberton calmly placed the muzzle of the gun in his mouth and fired once, instantly dying from a single shot to the head.

Far from being on the scene within 10 minutes of Julia picking up the phone, it was another 24 minutes before an unarmed team of police officers was dispatched. Even then, they had trouble locating the Pemberton's newly built home. As they pulled up outside the house, they spotted Will's body lying on the gravel drive. Despite attempts to give first aid, it was obvious he was dead. The officers then had to wait until an armed unit arrived to give back up, but it would still be another 6 hours before they were sufficiently convinced it was safe to enter the house. Inside they found the bodies of Julia and Alan, dead even before the first officers arrived on the scene.

How does a family rebuild itself after such a tragedy? How much time must elapse before the twin forces of passion and of rage that ripped them apart are once more fettered by everyday life? Julia's family, and particularly her brother, Frank Mullane, has thrown itself into campaigning for reforms in the way the police handle domestic violence. They have won a domestic homicide review into the killings in the hope that further investigation will help prevent the same thing happening in the future.

Alan's family is still trying to come to terms with what he did, and why, clinging to the image of him as a loving family man, driven over the edge by accusations of abuse and the prospect of losing everything he loved. Penny Cook – who found Alan's farewell letter, which included the comment that he'd hired a hit man to carry out the murder if he should fail – was left battling her own demons after her lover died. Though Alan had made sure she would be well provided for through his life insurance policy, she found herself haunted by unanswered questions. Could she have done more to prevent what happened? Should she have seen how fixated he was becoming? Why didn't she realise how dangerous he was?

What of Laura, who was the only one of the immediate family to escape the bloodbath? After burying her mum and brother one day, and her dad the next, she was left struggling to make sense of a crime that had taken every memory she'd ever had and torn it to shreds, the pieces swirling around her in the dead air like dust.

'We were a loving family,' she insisted, trying to claw back some fragment of what had been so cruelly taken from her. 'Words cannot express how I feel or how much I miss them.'

CHAPTER ELEVEN

MURDER IN THE LAND OF SMILES

Guy *forced himself to look up. His eyes widened with shock as he saw the gun pointing at him. He didn't understand, couldn't take in what he saw. His last thought, bizarrely, was that the silencer was as big as the gun.*

The girl slipped into the room. She was tiny with large brown eyes. She looked at the body on the floor and then at the man slipping the gun back into the waistband of his jeans. The expression on her face was of regret, sorrow and bewilderment. It passed quickly and she turned to Boy. 'Come on, Tilac, let's go,' he said. She gave him a quick, lop-sided smile and took his hand as they left the room.

★ ★ ★ ★ ★

As Toby Charnaud typed the last lines of what would turn out to be a top-prize winning short story, he had mixed feelings. On one hand he was pleased with how the story had turned out. He'd written it for a short story competition being run by a Bangkok magazine and it conveyed exactly the right tone of romantic wistfulness combined with tension and a brutal twist at the end. On the other hand, writing the story of a Western man who'd fallen in love with a beautiful Thai bar girl and given up everything to marry her only to realise she could never be loyal to him, brought up some painful memories.

So many of his personal feelings and experiences had been poured into that tale of a cross-cultural marriage borne out of optimism and love that ended in bitterness and betrayal. Still, he reflected, as he typed out the title 'Rainfall' on the coversheet, at least the ending – in which the wife had the hero killed – wasn't autobiographical. He and his own Thai ex-wife might still be embroiled in petty disputes over their divorce settlement and custody of their son Daniel, but thankfully their arguments stopped short of murder.

As Toby carefully slid the sheaf of papers on which his story was typed into the manilla envelope, like every aspiring writer he hoped his words would ring true for his readers. He wanted the characters he'd created to come to life on the page – their dialogue plausible, their actions credible. And he wanted readers to be able to relate to the feelings he wrote about and to imagine just how easily passion could turn poisonous. What he could never have imagined was just how sickeningly real his fictional creation would turn out to be.

★ ★ ★ ★ ★

For years now the Thai mail-order bride phenomenon has been big news and the older British man with the young Thai wife on his arm has become a comedy staple on TV programmes such as *Little Britain*. The Thais, too, have their own ways of mocking the male 'farangs' (white foreigners) who believe true happiness can be found for the price of an internet dating site subscription. The British Embassy in Bangkok processes around 70 applications a week from Britons wanting to marry Thai nationals – and most of these couples involve a considerable age difference, not to mention the sizeable cultural gulf created by a union where the two partners don't even speak the same language.

But the marriage of Toby Charnaud and Pannada Laoruang seemed to buck all the stereotypes. There was no massive age gap; the couple had had a proper courtship period. Above all, they were in love. When Toby first caught sight of Pannada in a bar in the Thai capital Bangkok, he was smitten. It was 1997 and, like thousands of adventurous Britons, the 33-year-old Chippenham man was enjoying a holiday in the exotic paradise of Thailand, Land of Smiles. Over the last decade he'd travelled all over the world –

America, Australia, Africa as well as Asia – meeting all kinds of people but there was something about the petite Thai girl working in the seedy Bangkok bar that drew him to her. When she came over to talk to him, there was a definite spark that made him forget the dinginess of the surroundings and the difficulties in communicating. All he saw was her soft brown eyes and the long shiny black hair that reflected the coloured lights from the bar.

Over the next few days, Toby and Pannada – known as 'Som', which means orange, to her friends and family – saw a lot of each other and by the time he went back to England, he felt a tug at leaving Thailand that he'd never experienced in the other exotic destinations he'd visited. Part of it was the country itself, the bustling city streets that gave out eventually to green jungles leading to palm-fringed white sandy beaches that seemed never-ending. But the other part was Pannada. Somehow the waif-like Thai girl with the fragile features had got under his skin. He just didn't want to leave her.

Back in the UK, thoughts of her weighed heavily on his mind. No matter how much he tried to tell himself it was just a holiday romance and couldn't go any further, he couldn't shake off the memories of the time they'd shared. Toby Charnaud, a burly, stocky former public schoolboy, was a man's man. Heavily into sport, he'd gone to agricultural college and then helped his parents run their prosperous Wiltshire farm. His was a masculine, practical, very English world. He'd never met anyone quite like exotic, dainty Pannada. Soon he was making plans to go back and see her, and in 1997 the couple were married in an exotic Thai wedding.

Most newly weds face their new lives with a certain amount of trepidation mixed with the excitement. How will commitment affect their relationship? What subtle alterations will marriage make to their daily lives? But when a marriage involves huge life changes for one or both partners, the anxiety becomes a hundred times worse. While Toby knew he was in love with his new bride, he was apprehensive about bringing her back to the Wiltshire village of West Kington with him. He knew his family – parents Jeremy and Sarah, plus his two sisters Hannah and Martha and brother Matt – would welcome anyone he loved into their lives. Nevertheless, it would be a massive culture shock for Pannada. She was leaving behind her family, her roots, everything familiar. Was it too much to ask of her?

On the surface of things, Pannada was getting the kind of opportunity girls in her position could only dream of. She had a man who adored her and could offer a life of luxury, such as she'd never imagined. Toby lived in a 6-bedroom manor house with stables and paddocks. For a girl from a poor Thai family, who'd been facing a future working in bars, vying with ever-younger girls to attract the attention of the male clientele, it was the stuff of fairytales. But bringing Pannada back to Wiltshire was like trying to grow an orchid in a daisy patch. The Charnaud family all tried their best to make the young Thai woman feel at home, but the unruffled pace of rural English life was in alien contrast to the adrenaline-laced bustle of the Bangkok streets. The relentless grey of the English weather weighed heavily on a spirit cultivated in the tropical warmth of the sultry Thai sunshine.

For two years, Toby Charnaud and his wife – now known to all as Som – tried hard to slot into the upper-class farming community in which Toby had been born and raised. He continued to run the family farm while she got a job in a nursery. But village life can be tough on outsiders, particularly where there's a language barrier as well, and although the couple made a few friends locally, they never really felt fully at home together. Alone in her sumptuous home, surrounded by rolling green lawns and mellow brick outbuildings, Som often felt that life as she knew it was going on somewhere else. The centuries-old manor house, with its vast, open fireplaces and wide oak floorboards, seemed to creak with a history pointedly not her own.

Som and Toby were keen to start a family. Nearly 30, she had already left it late by Thai standards, but she dreamed of bringing up a child under the familiar blue canopy of the Thai sky, surrounded by family and all that was familiar. 'I want to go home, Toby,' she told him, her shiny brown eyes gazing intently into his. 'I want to go back to

Thailand.' Toby, who'd travelled extensively all his life and understood the way a place could get under your skin, wasn't frightened by the idea of moving abroad. He loved his wife, he could see she'd made an effort to fit into his life. Now it was his turn to try to fit into hers.

In 1999 he sold his house in the UK. If they were going to begin a new life, he wanted to do it properly, with money behind them. They decided on moving to Hua Hin, an older-style beach resort 200 kilometres south of Bangkok on the West Coast of the Gulf of Thailand. Unlike some of the trendier Thai resorts, Hua Hin isn't known for its pumping rave music or all-night party scene. True, it boasts plenty of bars and restaurants, but they tend to attract an older, more settled type of visitor than better known rivals such as Koh Samui and Phuket. As an active fishing port, it has the year-round buzz of a working Thai town combined with the holiday feel of an upmarket resort.

Everything, from the Thai massages available on the long white sandy beach to the grand colonial architecture of some of the buildings, gives Hua Hin an air of laidback, understated luxury. And for keen golfer Toby Charnaud, the fact that it boasted 8 world-class golf courses within a 30-kilometre radius just added to the appeal. Surrounded by spectacular national parks with waterfalls, temples and jungle scenery, Hua Hin couldn't have been further removed from sleepy West Kington. Toby and Som believed it could offer them the new start they were hoping for. With a sense of true optimism, mixed with a healthy dose of apprehension, they bought a bar-restaurant complex on the beach. With Som's bar experience, they were confident they could make a go of the new business. For Toby, used to the punishing hours of farm management, the idea of a lazy round of golf in the afternoon followed by an evening socialising with the regulars in his own bar was seductively attractive.

For a while, it looked as though Hua Hin would be the paradise they'd been hoping for. The Rainbow Bar soon attracted a circle of regular expat clients and Toby became a popular member of the Handicap Committee at the Hua Hin Golfing Society. More importantly, Som was soon pregnant with their much wanted son, Daniel, who was born a year after their move to Thailand. The place abounds with horror stories of Westerners who fall in love with this most beautiful country – The Land of Smiles – and invest everything trying to make a life there only to end up losing the lot. Toby Charnaud, it seemed, was to be the exception. Unassuming and quiet, he nevertheless had a gentle humour that won him many friends in the town. People knew him as the kind of man who was just impossible to dislike. He had his golfing buddies, his regular bar customers, his lovely wife and now he had a son he completely and utterly adored. Really, he seemed to have cracked it. But life can sometimes have a habit of sneaking nasty surprises into even the sunniest of situations.

For the first time Som started to pull away from her

husband. She was living the life she'd always dreamed of with her son, her husband and a thriving business, but somehow it wasn't quite enough for the young, attractive woman. Part of her craved the kind of thrills her staidly prosperous new life couldn't provide. Unfortunately for her, she found what she was looking for in gambling.

Gambling is officially illegal in Thailand but that doesn't stop it being one of the most popular pastimes for a great many Thai adults. While some trek over the borders to play in the casinos of neighbouring countries like Cambodia, most indulge in small-scale betting through the widespread underground system. Thais will bet on anything – from card games to kickboxing bouts – and because it's not legal, there's no regulation of how money is paid out or collected. Unlike in the UK, where you place your bet upfront, quite often Thai betting is done on a book-system, where your bet gets recorded and if you win, you receive the difference between the amount you said you wanted to invest and the payout. If you lose, you're in debt to the bookies. The temptation then is to place another bet to try to recover the amount you owe, making it easy for debt to spiral out of control.

Like most Thais, Som started out placing small bets. She savoured the exquisite anguish of having to make a choice between different outcomes, weighing up all the possibilities before making a decision in a split-second splurge of adrenaline, in which excitement and doubt merged into one throat-choking ball of anticipation. And she relished the delicious, secret thrill that came with knowing she had a personal investment in how a card game or a football match ended up. 'Go on,' she'd urge under her breath, her brown eyes intently focused on the activity in hand. 'Go on, you can do it.'

Unfortunately for her, Som's gambling instincts weren't always entirely trustworthy and bit by bit, her debts began to mount. Panicking, she became caught up in that familiar gambler's paradox which says 'gambling might be how I ran up this debt, but it's also the easiest way to pay it off.' 'If I just win this next one, I'll stop,' she'd promise herself, during one of the high-stakes card games she played with increasing regularity. But if she did come out on top, she'd chalk it up to a winner's streak and convince herself she'd be mad to quit now – and if she lost? Well, how on earth was she going to pay the bookies back, if not by winning the next one?

Som kept the details of her mounting debts from her English husband. Toby was so proper, so law-abiding that he just wouldn't understand how it was possible to get such a kick from something so frivolous and so, well, dodgy. Perhaps it was just his public school upbringing coming to the surface, but sometimes he could be such an old stick-in-the-mud. In fact, Som was becoming just a little bit impatient with her kind, dependable husband. The flutters of excitement she got through gambling weren't enough to fully feed her need for thrills. In her old single life, she'd been used to attention from men – the appreciative glances, the tired chat-up lines. While she didn't exactly miss that life, there was some level where she still needed the validation she got from knowing she was desired, knowing she was attractive. Like many new mothers, she wanted to prove that the woman she had been was still there, somewhere outside the roles of mother and wife that threatened to overwhelm her life.

When a Thai policeman the couple knew started paying her attention, Som didn't discourage him. She was vulnerable and he was everything Toby wasn't. How far their relationship went isn't clear. But if Toby's prize-winning short story is as autobiographical as it appears, his wife wasn't about to let her marriage vows hold her back from experiencing the buzz she felt was lacking in her life.

Poor, gentle, kind-hearted Toby! He'd given up his family, his home, his heritage to follow his wife halfway round the world. They had a child together; they had a business together. He'd hoped and believed they had a future together. But as Som's behaviour became more furtive and remote, he saw that future melting away. For several months, he struggled to make things work. By nature he was not a quitter and he would have done anything to try to get things back to the way they were. 'Is there anything bothering you?' he'd ask Som, desperate to know the cause of the worry that now seemed permanently etched in her deep brown eyes.

Som herself was torn. On the one hand, she wanted to hang onto the financial and emotional security Toby offered. In her lifetime she'd seen too much poverty to hold any romantic notions about giving up everything for love or excitement. She wasn't ready to slip quietly into middle age, though. And then there was the matter of the mounting debts...

But Hua Hin is, ultimately, a small town. And as anyone who's ever lived in a small town will know, privacy is difficult to come by and secrets hard to keep. Rumours began to reach Toby's ears – places Som had been seen, places he wouldn't have expected her to be, things she said that didn't quite add up. With her emotional distance, his suspicions grew proportionately and soon their once easy, loving relationship became awkward and strained.

Psychologists who specialise in relationship counselling often talk about the 'elephant in the living room'. What they're referring to is the huge, unspoken issues that lurk ominously in many struggling couples' relationships. No matter how carefully you edge around them or step over them, no matter how studiously you try to ignore them, their presence still casts a huge, unmoveable shadow, blocking the way to any kind of resolution. For the Charnauds, Som's gambling addiction and need for extramarital excitement were the elephant in the living room.

While Toby remained in the dark, nothing he could do would make the situation any easier. He half knew there was some tumour growing inside his marriage, but didn't know how to find out what it was. As more snippets of information and gossip filtered through to him, the sickening realisation began to dawn. He and Som had a huge problem and confronting it would result in the destruction of the comfortable, pleasant life they'd built up for themselves. The fairytale would be over.

It's hard to live a normal life with a time bomb strapped to your back. Toby wanted his new life to work; he wanted his business to be successful, his son Daniel to grow up happy and loved by two parents, who also loved each other. But even while he was struggling on towards this utopian vision, he could hear the tickticking of an explosion waiting to happen. Eventually, heartbreakingly, the Charnauds' marriage crumpled under the weight of Som's secret double life and they separated. 'I just can't live with so many secrets,' Toby said sadly.

While tourists in the Rainbow Bar sipped Singha beers and admired the beauty of the setting sun away from the stresses of home, the bar's owners slowly and painfully picked their way through the wreckage of their relationship, trying to work out how to divide up what was left. According to their final divorce settlement in 2004, Toby paid Som a lump sum of £11,000 plus £6,100 towards her gambling debts. For his part, he retained ownership of the bar and, more importantly, was granted full custody of their son Daniel.

For a while following the divorce an uneasy truce existed between the two former lovers. Som moved to the countryside in the Petchaburi province about an hour away from Hua Hin and far enough removed from the temptations of the card games that cost her so dearly. Toby continued to run the bar and although Daniel lived with his father, he also saw his mother on a fairly regular basis. It wasn't the happy ending Toby had been hoping for when he'd married his beautiful Thai wife all those years before, but at least he still had his son and his business, his golfing buddies and his Thai dreams. Life could indeed be worse. If some balmy nights he lay awake wondering whether he could have done anything more to make his marriage work – if he looked into his son's eyes and momentarily saw his young bride once again standing before him – he learned to put those feelings aside. Instead he dedicated himself to building a new life for him and Daniel.

But Som was finding it harder to control her own feelings. Although the divorce settlement left her with a sizeable amount of money by Thai standards, it still wasn't enough to pay off her crippling gambling debts. She missed seeing her son, she missed the financial security she'd come to take for granted. Isolated in the countryside, she heard second-hand reports of what was happening in Hua Hin and how Toby was rebuilding his life without her, and she brooded on the unfairness of it. The thought of him meeting someone else and having more children, thus sidelining her even further, made her furious. How was it right that he got to carry on enjoying the same, easy-going lifestyle and high standard of living while she was exiled out in the sticks with her creditors breathing down her neck?

Owing money to the bookies in Thailand isn't a position you would want to find yourself in. As the industry is illegal, its methods of collection are unregulated and it's not uncommon for debtors to meet with nasty accidents or even mysterious deaths. Som needed money badly, but the only person she knew who had it was her ex-husband and he wasn't about to give her any of it. It was a shame, she reflected angrily, that he didn't meet with a nasty accident. Then all his money would go to Daniel and she, as Daniel's mother, would be in overall control.

Isn't it strange the way some thoughts that slip into your head so casually can take such a lethal hold? Try as she might, Pannada Charnaud couldn't rid herself of the idea that Toby's death would be the answer to all her problems. That way he could never go on to have more children, thus robbing her own son of his rightful fortune and, more pressingly, she'd be able to pay off all her considerable debts in one immensely satisfying swoop. It was such a seductive vision. In Som's eyes Toby's death would put right the injustices done to her by the divorce settlement. Once again she'd be at the helm of the bar business and she'd have her son. She'd be able to walk the streets without constantly looking over her shoulder in case one of her creditors had decided to send her a reminder message – by way of a baseball bat. With plenty of time on her hands, Som began to plan.

In March 2005, 5-year-old Daniel Charnaud went to see his mother. Although the terms of the divorce had granted Toby full custody, he knew how important it was for his son to retain links with his mother and his Thai heritage, so he'd encouraged such visits as much as possible. Som often had family staying from the impoverished Yasothon province where she'd grown up and it was good for the boy to speak Thai and learn more about his mother's roots.

On 27 March, Som asked Toby to come and pick up his son. When the quiet but friendly, golf-loving man left his home in Hua Hin, he thought he'd be back later that day to open up the bar as usual. Instead he disappeared. It was April before Som reported him missing, claiming he never turned up to collect his son and despite a cursory police investigation, no clues were discovered as to his whereabouts.

Back in Wiltshire, Toby's family became seriously concerned. He was normally such a reliable, hard-working person, it just wasn't in his character to take off without warning. They knew something must have happened to him. With an ever-growing knot of fear inside them, Toby's parents set about making enquiries over the internet about private investigators based in Thailand. To their relief they came across a Scottish PI now living in Bangkok. When they told him what had happened and voiced some of their concerns, he didn't seem too surprised. Despite its gentle image, Thailand has one of the highest murder rates in the world. He agreed to take on the case.

For Toby's anxious relatives, a nail-biting wait followed. People who've experienced what it's like to have someone they love go missing always talk about the impotence they feel. How much worse when you're 6,500 miles away, gazing at a phone that refuses to ring, hoping against hope to hear that one familiar voice saying, 'Sorry to worry you'. Or 'You'll never believe what just happened to me…' In the end when the phone finally did ring, it was the worst possible news. In direct contradiction to Som's claims that he'd never come to collect Daniel, mobile phone records revealed Toby had been in the vicinity of her country home on the day he went missing. This time, when police raided the house, they heard a very different version of events.

Present were two men, both relatives of Som's. They admitted to the police that they'd both been there the day Toby disappeared six weeks before, together with a third man, a neighbour of Som's. She herself had been at the market with her son Daniel. The story they told the police was so brutal and horrific that it would send shockwaves through Thailand's ex-pat community and haunt Toby's family for years to come. Initially the men's bizarre tale was that they'd grown angry at Toby for interrupting them while they were drinking whisky and killed him in a fit of anger. However, this account soon changed and it was claimed Som had hired the men to kill her husband, offering them £2,700 each if they were successful.

At first they'd tried to shoot him with a muzzle-loading hunting musket – an antiquated, cumbersome weapon – but when the musket jammed they beat him to death with an iron bar and wooden clubs. Quiet, good-natured Toby Charnaud who'd never hurt anyone had ended his life in the most brutal way possible. It was to get worse. After the killing, the men had tried to get rid of the body by dismembering it and barbecuing it, using 20 kilos of charcoal bought earlier that day. The charred remains were then distributed around the nearby Kaeng Krajan national park, a jungle-covered area known as home to some of Thailand's dwindling tiger population. In a sickening confirmation of their story, the men led the police straight to where the body parts had been dumped.

Som denied she'd hired the men. She claimed she'd come back from the market and found the body, and had helped them dispose of it but hadn't had any part in the actual killing. No one was buying her story: the only person who had anything to gain from the death of Toby Charnaud was his ex-wife.

On Wednesday 6 September 2006, Pannada Charnaud was found guilty of the brutal murder of her ex-husband and, along with the three men she'd hired to carry out the killing, sentenced to life imprisonment. For Toby's family back in Chippenham, it was the outcome they'd been hoping for. 'At last this chapter is closed,' said his father, Jeremy. Neither parent attended the trial, feeling unable to face sitting in the same courtroom as the woman they'd been convinced all along had taken the life of their beloved son.

Now Toby's son Daniel is cared for by his sister in Stanton St Quintin, Wiltshire, where he goes to the local school and enjoys the same things as any other 7-year-old English schoolboy – football in the playground on chilly winter days, ice cream in the park in the summer.

It's a very different upbringing to the one his father envisaged during the first years of Daniel's life, when Toby and Som were still together, running their bar in the pleasant heat of the South East Asian sun and planning their future life in Thailand, Land of Smiles.

CHAPTER TWELVE

FATHER OF THE YEAR

As the statuesque blonde approached, Darren Mack felt that familiar thrill of excitement. Toned to perfection with golden brown skin, she was obviously no stranger to the gym. Her breasts, straining against the plunging, clinging halter-neck top she was wearing, exhibited a give-away gravity-defying jut that owed more to a skilled surgeon than Mother Nature, but that didn't bother Darren at all. He was already enjoying the surge of adrenaline that came from knowing he would soon be exploring that body extremely intimately. 'And this is my husband,' the woman was saying, indicating the slightly awkward-looking man at her side.

While Darren reciprocated by introducing his own date

for the night, the woman's eyes never left him, passing slowly down his body and then up again. He felt himself instinctively tightening up his muscles, glad now of the hard work he'd put in on the weights machines. He knew he was looking good; he was in his element. This swingers' convention was turning out to be everything he'd hoped for – one of the best. If only the rest of his life could be like this, he reflected as the woman's hand lightly brushed his bulging upper arm, sending shivers of pleasure through him. It was so uncomplicated, so easy. Only his wife Charla and that crooked divorce judge were hell bent on screwing everything up for him. If it weren't for them, things would be just about perfect.

As the woman's hand rested once again on his arm before slowly moving lower… and lower… Darren tried to free his mind of negative thoughts. The divorce case was occupying far too much of his energy, he thought, nuzzling the woman's ear, his breath warm on her bronzed neck. It was energy that could be put to far better use. All he had to do was work out a way to get those two off his mind – and for good.

★ ★ ★ ★ ★

Darren Roy Mack was not the kind of guy to get on the bad side of. Not that he wasn't charming when he wanted to be, just that as the boss of a very successful family-run pawnshop business, he knew how to handle himself and he really, really didn't enjoy being told what to do. He liked to do what he wanted, when he wanted. No questions asked. Live and let live, that's what he believed.

By the age of 45, Darren had turned hedonism pretty much into an art form. Sure, he was a concerned and involved parent to his three children – two by first wife Debra and one by current wife Charla – but when he was off-duty, he liked to let rip – and why not? Co-owned with his mother, his pawnshop empire had made him very wealthy. He was his own boss, handsome in a very Rocky Balboa type of way and he believed absolutely in those two fundamental American rights: the pursuit of happiness and the freedom of the individual to make their own choices and live life their own way.

If self-gratification is your No. 1 aim in life, then Reno, Nevada is a pretty good place to be. Though the city has long since ceded the title of gambling capital of the world to its neighbour Las Vegas, it still boasts several top-class casinos plus a white-water park and hundreds of nightclubs and bars covering the entire range from upmarket right down to sleazeville. Outside of the city, the lakes and mountains offer a landscape often of breathtaking beauty but downtown it's a different story. Architecturally uninspiring, with its bland, modern buildings fronting onto wide, soulless, neon-studded streets, Reno's brash commercialism would hold little interest for those hooked on high-culture but for anyone with a healthy bank balance looking for unadulterated and unashamed 'fun', it's as good a place as any.

Over the years Darren had been a regular face at Nevada's legal brothels, particularly the infamous Moonlite Bunny Ranch. He loved the company of beautiful women and the excitement variety offers. For that same reason he also enjoyed attending swinging conventions, mass events usually taking place in some large, impersonal hotel, where broad-minded couples attend 'seminars' on all subjects erotica-related, plus a variety of anything-goes social bonding (and occasionally bondage) get-togethers. At first Darren's second wife, Charla, had gone along with his unconventional sexual mores and had even joined in. For Darren, who'd always been concerned about the image he projected to the world, Charla was the ultimate lifestyle accessory. With her long, wavy brown hair, falling carelessly to one side, dark, seductive eyes framed by long, black lashes and perfect, even smile, the former film actress added to his social cache. And the fact that she went along with his sexually progressive lifestyle just added to his sense of being a man who really did have it all. Darren Roy Mack was king of his world.

Perhaps in an attempt to counterbalance the hedonistic side of their relationship with something more spiritual, the couple became heavily involved with a movement known as the Landmark Education. Variously described by detractors as a 'cult', a brainwashing technique and a way of raising bucket loads of cash from emotionally vulnerable people, Landmark is also credited by its supporters with transforming lives and promoting individual and indeed world peace. Starting off with three-day courses aimed at encouraging participants to realise their true potential, Landmark is a mass self-awareness programme with different levels of involvement. Its claims of personal empowerment and promises of immediate results appealed to the Macks' go-getting philosophy and they lapped it up.

For a few years, the combination of sexual passion and a shared ambition to better themselves in every way made Darren and Charla Mack's marriage appear rock solid. To the outside world they were a pin-up couple – rich, good-looking, crazy about each other. Charla was a fantastic stepmother to Darren's two children and a doting mother to their own daughter Erika. Both she and her husband served on the school board. To those around them, unaware of Darren's sexual adventurism, they appeared the model family. In fact, in 1998 a billboard went up in Reno announcing 'The Mack Family Presents Darren Mack. 1998 Father/Husband of the Year. A unanimous decision by his wife, Charla, and his three wonderful children'.

Darren Mack had everything he wanted – the respect of his community, the love of his family and the excitement of sexual variety. He and Charla lived in a $1.2m Tudor-style mansion on Franktown Road in picturesque Washoe

Valley, 8 miles out of Reno itself. He drove a Hummer and treated himself to whatever state-of-the-art gadgets took his fancy. Darren was on top of the world. What his robust ego failed to consider was that when you're at the top, there's really only one way to go. Down.

After Erika's birth Charla grew less and less indulgent of her husband's broad sexual interests. Instead of looking outwards for adventure, she concentrated her energy on her family and their luxurious home. Erika and her half-brother and sister, Darren's children from his first marriage, became the centre of Charla's world. She loved being a stay-at-home mum and helping out at the kids' school; she just didn't need that thrill of pushing the sexual boundaries any more. Instead she was content with her home and her family and the fact that Darren wasn't became a bone of contention for the couple. 'Why aren't I enough for you?' Charla would rail at her husband.

They began to drift further and further apart. While they still had the passion that had brought them together in the first place, now they were just as likely to apply it to hurting, rather than loving each other. The chemistry between them was explosive but Darren frequently confided to friends that Charla could be physically and verbally abusive, although no one could believe he didn't give as good as he got. As he entered into his mid-forties, Darren still thought of himself as a player. Six years his junior, Charla was happy to be Mrs Mack, wife, mother and stepmother. It was increasingly obvious that something, or someone, was going to have to give.

In the end, it was the marriage that gave out. By 2004 the Macks, once the poster-family for the wealthy Nevada elite, were on the rocks. They agreed to separate, with Charla remaining in the Washoe Valley home and Darren taking up residence in a spacious condominium in a pale, terracotta coloured town house on Wilbur May Parkway, an exclusive housing development in South Reno. It's always a tragedy when a parent moves out of the family home. Can anything be more poignant than the dividing up of wedding presents or the grey marks on empty walls where once cherished photos hung? Is there any smell more exquisitely painful than the last sniff of a child's bedroom that will shortly be closed off to you, any sound more desolate than the click of what was once your own front door closing behind you?

Darren Mack did not want to give up his home and he certainly wasn't going to give up his daughter. When he walked away from Franktown Road he was determined that it was just a temporary measure. If Charla thought she was going to get everything her way, she had seriously underestimated him. At first, however, things did seem to be going in Charla's favour. After she filed for divorce in February 2005, Washoe Family Court Judge, Chuck Weller, ordered Darren to pay her temporary spousal support while the settlement was being worked out. She was also given temporary rights to live in the house and temporary custody of Erika.

For Darren, who prided himself on being an exemplary father, this last point was a particular blow. With Charla's help, he had fought a bitter divorce case with his first wife, during which he'd successfully won custody of their children. Now he was preparing to do the same again. He in turn asked the judge for temporary joint physical and legal custody of their daughter, plus possession of the home which, he argued, he had paid for.

As with so many divorcing couples, both partners were convinced they had the moral upper hand. Both believed themselves to be the best guardian for their child and to have the greatest entitlement to their family home. There is no more powerful adversary than someone convinced they are right.

In May 2005 Judge Weller ordered that Charla and Darren should share custody of Erika on a week-on, week-off basis. Usually the changeover would take place on a Monday so that one parent could drop Erika off at school in the morning and the other could collect her in the afternoon. A mutual restraining order was also put in place so that during the holidays, when the changeover had to take place at the Macks' private homes, contact was kept to a minimum. Whichever parent was dropping off the child should stay in the car, the order decreed, while the other remained inside their respective house.

Charla was given the right to remain in the Franktown Road home on the condition that it was put up for sale. Darren, whose earnings were put at around $44,000 a month, was ordered to pay the maximum allowable child support of $849 per month plus an extra $10,000 a month to cover household expenses while the house was being sold. He was furious. It seemed to him that Charla was just going to be allowed to sit pretty in the house that he was paying through the nose for, enjoying the Jacuzzi, the pool, the $10,000 television while he slaved away to pay for the upkeep of all those. She was still young, so why shouldn't she have to go out and get a job?

The divorce procedure got even nastier. Darren's mother, Joan Mack, sued Charla for the return of some jewellery that she claimed the younger woman had borrowed but Charla insisted had been gifts. In addition, Darren, who'd threatened Charla that he'd file for bankruptcy if she didn't accept his terms, went ahead and did just that. He'd made her a generous offer, he felt, and if she turned it down she'd get nothing. No one could make him pay his wife if he could show there were no funds to pay her with.

By August 2005 Darren had paid Charla just $9,000 of the nearly $40,000 alimony she was owed. He had got way behind on paying the bills and she and Erika had endured days without electricity or heating when the utilities were cut off. Only further legal action persuaded Darren to pay the $2,000 to get them turned back on again. Meanwhile, he immersed himself in the swinging lifestyle with newly single zeal. He spent hours working on his physique, pumping weights in the gym to build up his muscles. Most weekends he was off at conventions or holidaying with one female friend or another. The date his bankruptcy petition was filed he was at a swingers' party in Mexico, lounging by the hotel pool, topping up his already considerable tan.

He set up a MySpace account on the popular networking website under the username TooMuchFun. His profile showed a leather-jacketed Darren Mack declaring himself on the lookout for a 'beautiful, sensual, sexual, smart, fun woman with a respectful attitude'. And it wouldn't hurt either if the lucky lady didn't object to not being the only doll in the toy box, so to speak. So far he seemed to have no shortage of offers. He was on a roll; life was good. The only thorn in his side was Charla. It wasn't just the money for Darren made a lot and had a very healthy pension fund to fall back on. What really annoyed him was the idea that Charla believed she was getting one over on him – and that the American legal system seemed to be allowing her to get away with it.

In Nevada there was a growing movement of disaffected divorced dads, all angry at the way the divorce laws seemed designed to rob them of their rights as fathers, while still expecting them to stump up the money for their kids and their exes. Darren found himself increasingly in agreement with them. It was as if women thought that the biological accident of being mothers gave them the God-given right to grab hold of the kids and the family assets, while their poor chump ex-husbands worked themselves into the ground, bankrolling them for the rest of their lives. As a red-blooded American male it made him spit to think how some judge who didn't know a thing about him or his life could arbitrarily decide when he could see his daughter and what he should do with his money. But he knew there was little he could do to challenge the Court's temporary order. All he could hope for was that he and Charla could work out a more reasonable permanent settlement.

In January 2006 the Macks were back in the divorce court in front of Judge Chuck Weller. Over a tense period of time, they thrashed out a provisional settlement whereby Darren would pay Charla almost $1m over the following 5 years and his business would drop the charges against her as long as she returned the disputed jewellery. Also decided was the fate of various 'sex photographs' the couple had taken during their relationship and which were now in the possession of Charla Mack. According to the settlement they would now be destroyed.

At last it seemed as if this acrimonious marriage break-up was once and for all about to be settled. Judge Weller for one was mighty relieved. Arbitrating in a divorce case was always thankless, but this one had been harder than most. Darren Mack clearly had a deep-rooted problem with authority figures. He bridled visibly each time he was told to do something, and the looks he'd been shooting the judge… well, let's just say they weren't exactly full of professional admiration. The judge looked forward to ruling formally on the provisional settlement so that it could become the basis of the final divorce.

But over the next few weeks and months the hard-fought settlement began to crumble and corrupt under the acid onslaught of the Macks' mutual bitterness. Particularly contentious was the question of the litigation suit brought against Charla by Darren's mother. The terms of the settlement demanded not only that she should give up the idea of suing Charla over the missing jewellery, but also waive her right to sue her at any time in the future. Like her son, Joan Mack didn't enjoy being told what to do and, like many Americans, she believed in life, liberty and the right to litigate at the drop of a hat. She did not take kindly to the law trying to shield her daughter-in-law.

Meanwhile, Darren's already low opinion of the law hit rock bottom. He became convinced Judge Weller was heavily biased in favour of Charla. Why else was he trying to push through a settlement that was so blatantly unfair? Sure, Darren earned a lot of money, but by the time he'd paid Charla her $10,000 a month plus the mortgages on two homes and all household and childcare expenses, he was effectively well into the red. How on earth could that be justified? With each passing day, Darren grew more and more angry about what he believed to be a glaring miscarriage of justice. Now, in addition to his money-grasping estranged wife, he had another focus for his anger: Judge Weller.

He began trawling the internet trying to find records of any transgressions in the judge's past and he became convinced the judge was guilty of corruption, of passing rulings which favoured those who had contributed to his electoral campaign. Darren urged his friends and business acquaintances to join him to campaign against what he saw as the overt bias against fathers in the Nevada family courts. He started anonymous internet blogs in which he tried to ruin the judge's personal reputation.

By the time the Macks next appeared in front of Judge Weller in May 2006, the agreed settlement – just like the passion the couple once shared – had been ripped to shreds. Darren Mack was no longer prepared to accept the terms that had been worked out in January. He wanted to see a different judge and thrash out a whole new settlement under the guidance of someone he could be confident wasn't biased in his ex-wife's favour. But Judge Weller had had enough. 'I'm going to rule today,' he told the warring couple, giving them one last chance to try to reach an amicable agreement before he decided it for them. 'If we're going to have settlement discussions, the time to have them is before a ruling because I fear that by ruling, all I'm going to do is ignite a confrontation,' he warned them. 'One side's going to win, the other side is going to lose.'

It was a prophetic remark. Just three weeks later Charla Mack would suffer the greatest loss of all: the loss of her life.

The judge's ruling that day was that the agreement worked out in January should more or less stand as it was. Darren Mack had to keep his mother from pursuing a lawsuit against Charla, and Charla in turn would have to drop any thoughts of legal action against her mother-in-law or the business. On the financial side Darren now had 48 hours to come up with $480,000 and would then be expected to pay another $500,000 over the next 5 years. Furthermore a date was set for another custody hearing, as Charla wasn't happy with the arrangements regarding Erika.

Darren could hardly contain his anger as he listened to the judge's ruling. In essence, the way he saw it, Charla had won. All she had had to do, it seemed to him, was flutter her thick black eyelashes and flick her heavy mane of hair and the judge acceded to all her demands. Meanwhile, he – a hardworking, devoted father – had his legitimate concerns dismissed as if he was nothing. If there was one thing he couldn't stomach, it was being treated like a nobody. As he left the court, Darren threw the judge a look so murderous it seemed to poison the very air around it. Chuck Weller shivered. He was used to people being upset or disappointed at what he ruled, but he'd rarely come across someone so openly and aggressively hostile. At least that's the last I'll have to see of him for a while, he told himself, relieved.

How wrong he was.

If Darren Mack had been angry before the ruling, now his rage was out of control. His life had been whipped right out from under him, leaving him in total free-fall and there was nothing he could do about it. He felt completely impotent. Some guy who didn't know the first thing about him or his marriage had said a few words. Suddenly he'd gone from being a wealthy, respected businessman and full-time, involved father to a debt-ridden schmuck who'd be working all his life to pay for an idle ex-wife, who was perfectly capable of earning her own living, and a daughter he was only allowed to see half the time. Well, Judge Weller had picked the wrong man to mess with.

Darren stepped up his efforts to discredit the judge, calling everyone he knew in an attempt to whip up media interest and portraying himself as yet another loving father sacrificed on the altar of family court pro-women bias.

Meanwhile, Judge Weller began to notice strange things happening around him. There were odd noises around his house that remained unexplained. Then, early one Saturday morning in June 2006, he woke to find a mass of bikers on his property after someone – paying cash – placed an ad for a motorbike auction in the local paper, including directions to the judge's home and his phone number. Plus, a member of a fathers' rights group contacted him privately to warn him that a certain individual was campaigning tirelessly to ruin his professional reputation.

But if the judge realised he'd made a powerful enemy, he wasn't going to let it get to him. There's an agreement among lawyers that they'd rather litigate in any type of case than an acrimonious divorce because it's where emotions run highest and passions are most likely to spiral out of control with legal professionals trapped right in the middle. Catching the fall-out flak from an embattled couple was an unfortunate occupational hazard of any divorce lawyer. It came with the territory.

Darren Mack, however, didn't consider himself to be just another statistic. He was the centre of his own, highly important world – a world Judge Weller and Charla seemed hell-bent on destroying. He just couldn't get past the injustice of it all. This was America, for goodness sake! A man who worked hard all his life and did right by his kids ought to be lauded, not punished. Who did these people think they were?

On 7 June, Darren went to a local car-hire firm and rented a silver-coloured Ford Explorer. For a man who already possessed a Hummer and a Jeep Cherokee, it was an odd thing to do. But then again, Darren was always making trips here and there either on business or, more likely, pleasure. Maybe he wanted to save wear and tear on his vehicles or perhaps he just fancied a change. Who knew? Darren was very much his own boss.

On Sunday, 11 June 2006, Darren Mack phoned his old school-friend Dan Osborne, asking for a favour. The next morning was hand-over day and Darren asked if Dan could be there when Charla dropped off Erika and if he would then drive the girl to his mother's. Dan had known Darren for the best part of two decades and had roomed with him since his separation so he knew Erika well and treated the house as a home from home. He was also acutely aware of Darren's marital situation. It's a sad measure of the extreme emotions stirred up by divorce that a friend – who just two years before might have sat around a dinner table with a couple – would think nothing of being asked to prevent that same couple from doing one another physical or verbal harm now.

The following morning Dan Osborne turned up at his friend Darren's home at around 9am, as arranged. It was another hot, humid June day in Reno and in the early morning haze the Sierra Nevada mountains flanking the city already seemed blurry. As usual, the road outside Darren's house was deserted and the huge houses with their designer 'gardens' of perfectly kept plants growing out of grey stones and gravel seemed lifeless and rather flat, like cardboard cut-outs against the mountainous backdrop.

When Charla Mack's Lexus SUV pulled up outside the house a short while later and Erika came flying out the car, Darren asked his friend Dan to take the 8-year-old upstairs to watch TV while he went to talk to Charla about something. Before he walked out, he grabbed a paper bag. According to the terms of the restraining order, Darren shouldn't have gone out of the house, nor should Charla have left her car. If either one of them had stuck within the law, how differently might things have turned out for the Mack family.

Upstairs in the Wilbur May Parkway condominium, Erika was engrossed in television, but Dan Osborne was starting to feel uneasy. Darren had been outside for around fifteen minutes or more. What did he have to say that was so urgent? Besides, Dan's dog which he'd brought with him that morning was making a hell of a racket downstairs. Maybe it had got shut in somewhere, Dan guessed. He'd better go and find out what was going on. 'Won't be a minute,' he called to Erika, who barely glanced up from her programme.

Dan was just starting down the plush carpeted stairs when the door that leads from inside the condominium into the garage burst open. The dog flew in, clearly agitated. The distressed animal appeared to be wet and its owner was horrified to realise that its face, throat and feet seemed to be covered with blood obviously not its own. Following close behind was Darren Mack. Dan Osborne will never forget the expression on his old high school friend's face as he came in from the garage. Darren had a 'weird look', he would later tell investigators. It was as if he was scared of something, or had been scared by something. He also had a towel wound round one hand.

After Darren climbed wordlessly up the stairs and disappeared into his bedroom, Dan Osborne became, in his own words, 'freaked out'. Ushering Erika and the dog down the stairs and outside, he bundled them quickly into his car. His heart was thudding as he turned the ignition key trying to maintain his composure so as not to worry the little girl whose life, though she didn't know it yet, would never be the same. Charla's car was still in the driveway but there was no sign of the beautiful, vibrant actress. Dan had no idea what had just gone on but two things were very clear in his mind: he had to get Erika to her grandmother's and something very wrong had happened in that house.

Dan was well into the 20-minute drive to Joan Mack's when his mobile started to ring. 'Hey Dan, it's Darren. Why'd you leave so soon? How about going for a coffee with me?' If Dan Osborne heard any strain in his friend's voice he tried hard to convince himself of a reasonable explanation. Perhaps he'd cut himself while in the garage or maybe he'd spilled a tin of red paint. When Darren suggested they meet right away in a local Starbucks, Dan was relieved. How awful could things be if Darren was meeting up with him for a coffee? He must have been imagining things, he told himself.

Coffee was a fairly subdued affair but with the week stretching ahead in all its oppressive monotony Monday morning meet-ups can often be so. But, as Dan Osborne left Starbucks to continue on his way to Joan Mack's house, he was once again assailed by the unshakeable feeling that something was seriously awry with his good friend Darren. Delivering Erika to her grandmother's house, he shared his concerns with Darren's mum. The blood on the dog, the expression on Darren's face, the towel around the hand, the fact that he'd changed his clothes before coming out for coffee – it just didn't add up. Or rather it did, but not in any way either of them wanted to believe. Darren wouldn't have done anything to Charla, they told themselves. Sure, things had got nasty between them but that was normal in any divorce. Darren was a great guy; he didn't have it in him to hurt anybody.

But shortly after 11am Dan received a call from a friend that lent sickening weight to all his unthinkable suspicions. Chuck Weller, the judge Darren had been waging a public hate campaign against, had just been shot by an unknown sniper. At 11.11am, with a heavy heart Dan Osborne called the Emergency Services, asking them to investigate a possible incident on Wilbur May Parkway. When the police arrived 20 minutes later at Darren Mack's house, they found it deserted. All the doors were locked and there was no sign of Charla's Lexus, which Dan reported being parked on the driveway. The police had no search warrant so they couldn't enter the property and all they could do was assume that at some point over the last couple of hours Charla Mack had got back into her car and driven away.

Besides, the city's Emergency Services had a bigger story on their hands than a missing woman. The shooting of a judge in government buildings in broad daylight was headline material.

Judge Chuck Weller had been standing at the window of his third-floor office in the County Courthouse just after eleven when there was a horrific cracking sound. The glass pane exploded into tiny fragments and the judge hit the floor as a bullet ploughed into his chest. One of the judge's terrified staff was also hit by shrapnel fragments as she cowered on the ground although her wounds later turned out to be superficial. Still alive, the judge was rushed in agony to the nearest hospital but his immediate concern was for the safety of his wife, Roza. If the same person was responsible for the shooting as had placed the motorcycle auction ad the week before, they knew exactly where he lived. 'Tell Roza to leave the house!' gasped the 52-year-old judge.

Back at the courthouse experts were poring over the evidence. Signs were that this was a meticulously executed assassination attempt. The sniper appeared to have fired from a parking garage above a cinema complex that was some way from the courthouse yet retained a direct view of it. But who would have wanted Judge Chuck Weller dead? And who had the resources, the know-how and the sheer motivation to carry such a plan through?

Of course, as with any courtroom judge, there was any number of disgruntled former plaintiffs who might have wished the judge ill – people unhappy at having to pay too much to their exes or share custody of their children. But not many had actively proclaimed their animosity. The judge's flustered staff presented police with a shortlist of people who had a particular axe to grind. Among the names was Darren Mack.

By 1.30pm detectives were back in touch with Dan Osborne. This time they were taking his concerns about Charla Mack's welfare extremely seriously. When they went back to Wilbur May Parkway they had the code to open the garage door. Hardened by years of watching detective movies, most of us imagine police attending the scene of a potential crime to be adrenaline-pumped automatons, carrying out the well-learned drills with blank-minded efficiency. In reality, though, poised before a closed door, there's a moment when thoughts of what you might find inside flash through your mind like projected images on an empty wall.

The first thing police officers noticed when the garage door finally slid smoothly open was Charla Mack's Lexus SUV parked inside. Next, her body, wearing blue trousers and a red top, lying face down in a pool of blood.

A search of Darren's house yielded various items of clothing, all stained with red, plus more than 50 boxes of ammunition, 4 empty rifle cases and documents detailing Judge Chuck Weller's campaign contributions as well as literature from fathers' rights groups. They also found, in the master bedroom, the sheath from a knife.

The most bizarre discovery was what looked to be a 'to do' list which appeared to be a list of instructions including:

Dan take Erika to Joan

Garage door open

End problem

Put lex in garage/lock home

parking garage if yes

Could Darren really have written himself out a list of step-by-step instructions for carrying out a double murder?

The one person no one could find was Darren Mack himself.

A few minutes after the shooting of Judge Weller, Darren's cousin, Jeffrey Donner, had received a call on his mobile. Listening to Darren ranting about what he believed to be the corruption of the family court system, Jeffrey wasn't unduly worried. After all, Darren had been spouting this stuff for the last year or so. He'd heard it all before. But then his cousin had said something that made him sit up and take notice. 'If anything should happen to me, please make sure the true story about the injustices that are going on in that courtroom get out to the media and the public.'

It was a strange thing to say but the conversation was over before Jeffrey really got a chance to ask his cousin what he meant. And that was the last anyone heard from him for the next 10 days. As far as the authorities and his family were aware, outspoken, fast-living Darren Roy

Mack had quite simply disappeared. For over a week authorities in the US mounted a huge manhunt for the millionaire pawnshop owner. In stark contrast to his 'Father of the Year' billboard, Darren's face was now plastered over newspaper front pages and the FBI's most wanted list. All over America, people claimed sightings of him but gradually the search was narrowed down to Mexico, the place Darren had used as a pleasure playground on several of his frequent romps away.

Back in Reno, evidence was accumulating that only increased the authorities' determination to bring Darren Mack in for questioning. Surveillance cameras in the parking lot near the courthouse showed the shots that hit Judge Weller had most likely come from a silver vehicle similar to the one Mack had rented the week before. An examination of Charla's body revealed 7 stab wounds, the most severe being to the neck and chest. Her mobile phone and a few other things were found scattered along interstate I-80 Westbound from Reno.

Puerto Vallarta, on the West Coast of Mexico, is a prosperous seaside resort known for its relaxed atmosphere and stunning landscapes. It's where the wealthy upper classes from nearby Guadalajara have their beach houses. While not as relentlessly built up as somewhere like Cancun, it's a far cry from the fishing village it once was which John Huston chose for the setting of his controversial 1963 film *The Night of the Iguana*, starring

Elizabeth Taylor and Richard Burton. It was a great choice for someone looking to blend in with a crowd, but avoid the most obvious tourist destinations.

Darren Mack liked Mexico and he liked Puerto Vallarta. He felt at home there, whether on the sandy beaches of Banderas Bay, or at one of its many upmarket bars and restaurants. If you were embarking on what could be your last days of freedom, you might do worse than enjoy them here, sipping cocktails at a seafront bar, or watching the yachts bobbing up and down on the crystal blue waters of the Pacific. But Darren realised the net was tightening. The authorities had traced phone calls he'd made back to bus stations in Western Mexico. Roadblocks had been set up and vehicles searched. He knew the authorities were on his tail and that if he waited to be arrested by Mexican police, he might end up spending time in one of the infamously inhospitable Mexican jails. His options were dwindling fast. On Thursday, 22 June 2006, he announced through his Reno attorneys that he was ready to give himself up.

The following day he was flown to Dallas, where he was arrested for the murder of his wife Charla. That night he arrived back in Nevada, touching down at Reno–Tahoe International airport just after 11.30pm.

The crowds who'd waited up to see him, expecting the cocky figure from the press reports with the dazzling white smile and neatly gelled hair, were disappointed. Darren's distinctively long, jutting chin was covered by a dark patchy beard. He appeared to have put on weight as if he'd been bulking up too fast in the gym or taking too many steroids. In place of the leather jacket was a crumpled navy T-shirt with contrasting orange sleeves. The characteristic arrogant swagger had been replaced by a more diffident step as he was ushered through the airport, shackles round his wrists and a startled look in his red-rimmed eyes. 'Is that really him?' people whispered anxiously.

Since then, Darren Mack has sat in a Reno jail awaiting trial, charged with murdering his wife and attempting to murder Judge Chuck Weller. The man who once prided himself on his smart appearance has swapped designer clothes for a prison-issued jumpsuit. Though prosecutors are not pushing for the death penalty, the 'player' who once lived for pleasure faces the prospect of a life behind bars.

The case has inflamed public opinion in Reno, where a vocal minority believe him to be a devoted father pushed beyond the limits of his endurance by a greedy ex-wife and a deeply unjust divorce system. Others view him as a control freak who couldn't cope when things didn't go his way.

Darren Mack himself has pleaded not guilty to all charges. From his jail cell, he continues to insist on being the choreographer of his own life, fighting any financial claims made by lawyers for Charla's estate. His MySpace page indicates that he or someone close to him last accessed it on 23 June 2006, the day he was arrested. Although various friends of his have kept it updated, the page with its now ironic 'TOOMUCHFUN' moniker remains an eerie shrine to long-gone hedonism. Like his 'real life', it appears frozen in time the day the handcuffs went on.

As Reno life carries on around him, as the croupiers deal cards in the casinos and customers queue at the cash desk in the pawnshop his mother still runs, the question lingers unanswered in the sultry city air:

Did Darren Mack destroy his family and his future? Or did divorce and the system that surrounds it destroy Darren Mack?